# The IC Chef Cookbook

A Collection of More Than 260 Bladder
& Prostate Friendly Recipes
Shared By Patients Just Like You!

Edited by Jill Heidi Osborne MA
President & Founder

Interstitial Cystitis Network
www.ic-network.com

**The IC Chef Cookbook**
Copyright 2015 © Interstitial Cystitis Network
All rights reserved.
ISBN: 978-0-9797840-0-2

**Publisher**
Interstitial Cystitis Network - www.ic-network.com
PO Box 2159, Healdsburg, CA USA 95448
1-800-928-7496 or 1-707-538-9442

Published in 2015
Produced and printed in the USA

To order a copy of this book, please visit: www.icnsales.com

**Writer & Editor**
Jill Heidi Osborne MA (jill@ic-network.com)

**Image Credits**
*Courtesy of istockphoto*
Cover: © -101PHOTO-
*p. 6 © Stockphoto24*
*p. 17 © iodrakon*
*p. 21 © Karcich*
*p. 27 © caroljulia*
*p. 31 © ShyMan*
*p. 45: © jreika*
*p. 49 © Sarsmis*
*p. 53 © AWEvans*
*p. 59 © StephanieFrey*
*p. 63 © elenakor*
*p. 70 © RuthBlack*
*p. 99 © milosluz*
*p. 101 © YelenaYemchuk*

**Disclaimer**
The Interstitial Cystitis Network, a division of J.H. Osborne Inc., is not a medical authority nor do we provide medical advice or medical services. No information written or implied in this book, the IC Network websites, videos, newsletters and magazine, or any resource suggested, should be considered medical advice. Only a licensed medical care provider should provide medical advice to you. Rather, our goal is to educate so that you can learn more about the subject and engage in a meaningful dialogue with your personal medical care providers. Please contact your physician for information regarding any change you wish to make in your lifestyle. The Interstitial Cystitis Network urges you to carefully research ANY information that you find regarding your health and wellness, including information received from the IC Network, Jill H. Osborne or associated entities.

**Trademark Notice**
Throughout this book various trademarked names are used. In the interest of our readers, we are using these names in an editorial fashion. In the interest of the trademark holders, we cite their ownership of the trademarks, with no intention of infringement.

# Dedication

No discussion of the IC diet can begin without the well-deserved acknowledgement of five special women.

**Bev Laumann** was on her way to a career in science when her IC struck. Undaunted, she applied those skills to IC outreach by running the Orange County IC Support Group and authoring the first book on the IC diet, **A Taste of the Good Life: A Cookbook for an IC Diet**. For many years, Bev also contributed a feature column to the IC Network website, *"Fresh Tastes by Bev,"* a collection of more than fifty articles on food and IC. What makes Bev truly special is her keen understanding of the science behind food, the use of preservatives, flavorings and so forth. She is one of the most educated and informed IC activists in the world.

**Julie Beyer MA, RDN** was the first registered dietitian to make the case that food could influence bladder health to the national dietitian community, traveling around the country educating nutrition professionals about interstitial cystitis and the unusual relationship that we have with certain foods. Despite their often harsh questions about the lack of research (now moot), she fearlessly shared her personal experience as an IC patient and the stories of many others who found themselves struggling with severe pain after eating certain foods. Julie has also answered questions about the IC Diet in the ICN Support Forum for more than a decade. Julie is the author of three books dedicated to the IC Diet: **Confident Choices®: Customizing the IC Diet, Confident Choices®: A Cookbook for an IC and OAB** and **Interstitial Cystitis: A Guide for Nutrition Educators.**

**Barbara Shorter MS, MEd, EdD** is an associate professor of nutrition at Long Island University and the Smith Institute of Urology. She developed and conducted several research studies that have proven the connection between food, interstitial cystitis and, most recently, chronic prostatitis, including the ground breaking study *"Effects of Comestibles on Interstitial Cystitis/Painful Bladder Syndrome"* published in the *Journal of Urology*. Barbara, too, has IC and also provides nutrition counseling to patients at the Smith Institute.

For more than a decade, **Diane Manhattan Lopresti** was the assistant manager of the ICN Support Forum. Each day, despite her own bladder symptoms, she spent hours helping others. I asked Diane to organize and solicit recipes the ICN's on-line IC Chef Cookbook and she poured herself wholeheartedly into the task, amassing a wonderful collection. Her spirit lives on through the many IC patients she befriended.

The ultimate foodie, **Carole** gently stepped into Diane's role and, for the past several years, has developed a now fabulous collection of recipes. One of our best and longest serving volunteers, Carole clearly loves to cook and tweak recipes so that they are bladder friendly. You'll find dozens of her recipes in this cookbook!

Thank you Bev, Julie, Barbara, Diane and Carole for all that you have done to help the IC community. We are blessed by your activism!

# Foreword

Although interstitial cystitis was identified over 130 years ago, it wasn't until the advent of the Internet that patients could share information about IC, their diagnoses, treatment and, especially, diet with people all over the world. In fact, we can directly trace the acceptance of food as an IC trigger and the eventual inclusion in the AUA treatment guidelines for IC/BPS to the vast amount of information patients have shared with each other over the past two decades. Not surprisingly, these anecdotal reports of foods irritating our tender IC bladders were eventually confirmed in a variety of research studies proving that we, the IC patient, have considerable insight and experience to offer.

For the past twenty years, Jill Osborne and the thousands of members of the Interstitial Cystitis Network Forum (www.ic-network.com/forum) have shared their journeys with interstitial cystitis, including the recipes you find in this book. This cookbook is a celebration of that wisdom and, more, importantly the empowerment that patients experience when collaborating with each other.

For those patients asking *"what can I eat without irritating my bladder,"* this book is full of ideas. From Nomato Sauce that is a bladder friendly alternative to tomato based pasta sauce to finding a satisfying alternative to coffee or green tea, there are low acid options that work and work well! Ingredient substitutions do not mean that quality suffers. You can enjoy some of your favorite flavors again with just a little bit of creativity.

Just remember that every patient has different food tolerances. You will, most likely, be adapting many of these recipes for your own unique tolerances. If you see a recipe that you'd like to try but it contains an ingredient that you're not sure of, just leave it out or look for a less intense substitute. Vinegar, for example, can be swapped with blueberry or pear juice. If onions bother you, try chives. Lemon juice may be swapped with a little bit of lemon zest. If you crave chocolate, try white chocolate or carob instead! I encourage you to play with flavors! You can enjoy cooking and meals again! Thank you, IC patients past and present, for sharing your tasty treats with us all.

- Julie Beyer RD (Author of **Confident Choices®: A Cookbook for IC & OAB, Confident Choices®: Customizing the IC Diet & Interstitial Cystitis: A Nutrition Guide for Educators**)

## Honor Roll of Awesome Patients

| | | |
|---|---|---|
| AgilityMe | icnmgrjill | Rawestrus |
| Angeles | Icyjunomary | Robin |
| aprilchen | Jenn | sandberg4 |
| Barbm | Jennybird | Sarah1982 |
| bbear | Jinny Jean | sasapippi |
| Bladderella | Just1ofamillion | Shawnster |
| Blazer | Jwlrs | sdm |
| Briza | Kadi | soupey28 |
| beverlyann | Kagey | Squirrel |
| Carole | KellyB | Stacey79 |
| CBZ1982 | Ktmeak7 | sunflower23 |
| Cgoheen | leelee | SweetPea85 |
| clevsea | Lisa7688 | Tectonic |
| cmcnatt | Lizzylu | Treekangaroo |
| durangomandy | LovesLife | valkay18 |
| Daisy | Mareng9 | Verdicries |
| DawnGrace | Marmotte | Wagamama |
| Diane M | Missisola | wcrox |
| Egrolman | mrmambo | wheresmysmokes |
| emilyandlouise | mystereys | |
| Emily3wst | n2indigoky | |
| flowergirl | Nekura | |
| fmcbride | nihon | |
| GayleK | Ollie R | |
| Hazel | Percy | |
| HRJ | Phoenixgirl | |
| Hnull2007 | RaiinbowEyes | |

# Table of Contents

Introduction ........................................................................................................................... 1

How Foods & Chemicals Irritate The Bladder .................................................................... 1

Ingredients Which Often Cause Problems ........................................................................ 2

The IC Food Lists ............................................................................................................... 3

    (A) The LIU Food Lists ................................................................................................... 4

    (B) The ICN Food List ................................................................................................... 4

About The Recipes ............................................................................................................. 4

Abbreviations & Substitutions ........................................................................................... 5

Beverages ........................................................................................................................... 6

  HOT DRINKS ..................................................................................................................... 6

    White Chocolate Vanilla Bean "Cocoa" w/ Cinnamon Whipped Cream (n2indigoky) ................... 6

    Karen's Vanilla Steamer (kagey) ............................................................................................ 6

    Karen's Hot Drink Topping (kagey) ......................................................................................... 6

    Vanilla Herbal Coffee (lizzylu) ................................................................................................ 6

    Hot Butterscotch (GayleK) ..................................................................................................... 6

    Steamed Almond Milk with Carob (jwlrs) ................................................................................ 6

    White Hot Chocolate (percy) .................................................................................................. 7

    White Peppermint Hot Chocolate (Carole) .............................................................................. 7

    White Peppermint Patty (Soupey28) ...................................................................................... 7

    Delicious Hot Caramel (ktmeak7) .......................................................................................... 7

    Hot White Chocolate (Diane M) .............................................................................................. 7

    Honey Tea (fmcbride) ............................................................................................................. 7

    Hot Milk with Maple Syrup (DawnGrace) ................................................................................ 7

    Starlight Mint (DawnGrace) .................................................................................................... 7

    My Favorite Pumpkin Pie Latte (Daisy) ................................................................................... 8

    Hot Pumpkin Pie Milk Drink (icyjunomary) ............................................................................. 8

    Dulce De Leche (Angeles) ...................................................................................................... 8

    Peanutbuttery Butterscotch Dream (OllieR) ........................................................................... 8

    Coconut Cream Caramel (Carole) .......................................................................................... 8

    Pear Cider for the Sweet Tooth in You! (OllieR) ...................................................................... 8

    Eggnog Latte (LovesLife) ........................................................................................................ 9

    Chocolate Coconut Cream (Carole) ....................................................................................... 9

    Mexican Hot "Carob-cocoa" (loveslife) ................................................................................... 9

    Mocha Free Mocha Latte (loveslife) ....................................................................................... 9

    Yummy Hot Carob Drink (Marmotte) ...................................................................................... 9

    Carob Mocha Powdered Mix (Marmotte) ............................................................................. 10

    Peppermint & Chamomile Tea with Honey (flowergirl) .......................................................... 10

Karen's Hot Cinnamon Tea (kagey)...............................................................................10

Caffixiccino Recipe (beverlyann).................................................................................10

SHAKES & CREAMY DRINKS ..........................................................................................10

Homemade Almond Milk (Briza)..................................................................................10

Eggnog (Carole)...........................................................................................................10

Homemade Shamrock Shake (Jennybird).................................................................10

Blueberry Cobbler (Carole).........................................................................................11

Healthier Alternative to Milkshakes (Kadi)...............................................................11

Candy Cane Drink (Carole).........................................................................................11

Protein Shake (Barbm) ...............................................................................................11

Coconut Pear Shake (Jinny Jean)...............................................................................11

Coconut Milk Shake (Carole)......................................................................................11

CaroNut Shake (OllieR)...............................................................................................11

Blueberry Milk Shake (lizzylu)....................................................................................12

ICED & SWEET TEAS.........................................................................................................12

Chamomile Honey–Vanilla Iced Tea (Lizzylu) .........................................................12

Sweet Mint & Basil Iced Tea (lisa7688) ...................................................................12

Mint Ice Tea (Shawnster).............................................................................................12

Bottled Cinnamon Mint Tea (blazer 55)....................................................................12

ICED COFFEE & COFFEE SUBSTITUTES...........................................................................13

Vanilla Iced Coffee (hnull2007)..................................................................................13

Fake Mocha Latte (treekangaroo)..............................................................................13

FRUIT SMOOTHIES ...........................................................................................................13

Smoothies by Kadi .......................................................................................................13

Strawberry Shortcake Smoothie (Carole).................................................................13

Breakfast in a Glass (Carole)......................................................................................13

Banana Natural Peanut Butter Smoothie (aprilchen) ............................................14

Melon Juice (OllieR).....................................................................................................14

Watermelon Icee (mystereys)......................................................................................14

Pear Juice Freeze with Ginger and Vanilla (wagamama).......................................14

HERBAL & VEGGIE ...........................................................................................................15

Sports Drink (sdm)........................................................................................................15

Cucumber Basil Water (durangomandy)...................................................................15

Infused Juice (Blazer)...................................................................................................15

Peppermint water (cmcnatt)........................................................................................15

Green Juice (kadi).........................................................................................................15

ALCOHOLIC........................................................................................................................15

Coco Nut Martini (blazer 55).......................................................................................15

Hawaiian Hazelnut (hnull2007) ..................................................................................16

Breakfast & Brunch...........................................................................................................17

PANCAKES & FRENCH TOAST ........................................................................................17

Baked Blueberry French Toast (Bladderella) ...............................................................17

Old Fashioned Pancake Recipe (Carole)...................................................................17

German Pancakes (Carole) .......................................................................................17

Cinnamon Peach Pancakes (Carole) ........................................................................18

Ricotta-Cottage Cheese Pancakes (Diane M) ...........................................................18

Stuffed French Toast (Diane M) ...............................................................................18

Rockin French Toast (Ollie R)...................................................................................18

Gluten, Egg, and Dairy Free Blueberry Pancakes (Sarah1982) ...............................18

Simple Pear Brunch (Blazer) ....................................................................................19

**QUICHE & EGG DISHES** .........................................................................................**19**

Vegetarian Quiche (Squirrel) ....................................................................................19

Asparagus Quiche (Carole) ......................................................................................19

Broccoli Quiche (Carole) ..........................................................................................19

Egg Scrambles (Kadi) ..............................................................................................20

Mini Frittatas (stacey79) ...........................................................................................20

# Burgers, Sandwiches & Pizza .........................................................................21

Chicken Burgers (mareng9) ......................................................................................21

Steak Sandwich (Kadi)..............................................................................................21

Grilled Peanut Butter Apple Sandwich (Carole) ........................................................21

Grilled Bacon Apple Sandwich (Carole) ...................................................................22

Ham and Pear Sandwich (Carole).............................................................................22

Beets, Spinach, and Goat Cheese Sandwich (Carole)..............................................22

Bean Cakes in Lettuce Wraps or Corn Tortillas (Briza).............................................22

Greek Gyros (Raiinbow Eyes) ..................................................................................23

Japanese Onigiri – Rice Balls (Nihon) ......................................................................24

Mini Pizza's (SweetPea85)........................................................................................24

Easy Whole Wheat Pizza Dough (Bladderella) .........................................................24

Nomato Pizza Sauce (Carole) ..................................................................................25

Spinach Sesame Pizza (sasapippi) ...........................................................................25

Crustless Veggie Pizza (Diane M) .............................................................................25

Pizza with a Creamy Garlic Sauce  (Carole) .............................................................25

Creamy Feta Pizza Sauce (missisola) .......................................................................26

Watermelon–Pepper Pizza Sauce (mrmambo)..........................................................26

# Sauces, Marinades, Relish & Jelly ................................................................27

**SAUCES & GRAVY** .................................................................................................**27**

Alfredo Sauce (Carole) .............................................................................................27

Homemade Enchilada & Taco Sauce (Bladderella) ...................................................27

Red Bell Pepper Sauce (Phoenix Girl).......................................................................27

Roasted Orange Bell Pepper and Garlic Sauce (Briza) .............................................28

Creamy Cauliflower Sauce (Bladderella) ...................................................................28

Raisin Sauce To Serve With Ham (Carole) ..................................................................28

Mushroom Gravy (agilityme) ..................................................................29

Nomato Sauce (loveslife) ..................................................................29

Nomato Ketchup (loveslife) ..................................................................29

**MARINADES, RELISH & JELLY** ..................................................................29

Root Beer Meat Marinade (Carole) ..................................................................29

Non-Cranberry Thanksgiving Relish (sunflower23) ..................................................................29

Cabbage Condiment (Carole) ..................................................................30

Easy Blueberry Jelly (HRJ) ..................................................................30

## Main Dishes ..................................................................31

**FISH & SEAFOOD** ..................................................................31

Shrimp & Scallops in a Buttered Garlic Sauce (Carole) ..................................................................31

Chamomile Poached Tilapia (mareng9) ..................................................................31

Easy Shrimp Scampi (Bladderella) ..................................................................31

Crispy Coconut Shrimp (Carole) ..................................................................32

Sinful Salmon (HRJ) ..................................................................32

Tuna or Salmon Burgers (Diane M) ..................................................................32

Baked Fish with Almond Stuffing (Diane M) ..................................................................32

Salmon Loaf (Diane M) ..................................................................33

**POULTRY** ..................................................................33

Turkey and Apple Meatloaf (wagamama) ..................................................................33

Chicken Broccoli Alfredo (Bladderella) ..................................................................34

Turkey and Rice Bake (Carole) ..................................................................34

Chinese Almond Chicken (Kadi) ..................................................................34

Light and Easy Chicken and Dumplings (Briza) ..................................................................34

Pizza Chicken (Carole) ..................................................................35

Chicken Fajitas with Roasted Red Peppers (Bladderella) ..................................................................35

Chicken Casserole (Diane M) ..................................................................36

Low Fat IC Friendly Turkey Meatloaf (CBZ1982) ..................................................................36

BBQ Chicken (Carole) ..................................................................36

Grilled Chicken with Cucumber Yogurt Sauce (Raiinboweyes) ..................................................................37

White Chicken Chili (mrmambo) ..................................................................37

Chicken Fricassee (Diane M) ..................................................................38

Portobella Mushroom Chicken (valkay18) ..................................................................38

Quinoa Pilaf with Chicken (Carole) ..................................................................38

Yummy Chicken (just1ofamillion) ..................................................................39

Chicken & Veggie Kebabs (Kadi) ..................................................................39

**BEEF** ..................................................................39

Stuffed Meatloaf (Carole) ..................................................................39

Beef Hash & Cabbage (cgoheen) ..................................................................39

Sizzling Steaks with Toasted Garlic Sauce (Diane M) ..................................................................39

Beef Rib Eye Roast w/ Potatoes, Mushrooms, and Fancy Pan Gravy (Diane M) ..........................40

Flank Steak and Roasted Cauliflower with Yogurt and Cilantro (rawestrus) ...........................40

Shepherd's Pie with Homemade Cream Corn (Carole) ...........................................41

PORK ...........................................................................................41

Stuffed Pork Chops (Carole) ....................................................................41

Sausage and Potato Foil Packet (Carole) .......................................................41

Pork Loin in the Crockpot with Butternut Squash (HRJ) ........................................41

Maple Encrusted Pork Chops (Carole) ..........................................................42

Easter Ham (Carole) ...........................................................................42

Pork Chops with Pears or Apples (Briza) .......................................................42

VEGETARIAN .................................................................................42

Zucchini Rice Gratin (mareng9) ................................................................42

Vegetarian Shepherds Pie (agilityme) ...........................................................43

Red Beans and Rice (Briza) .....................................................................43

Mushroom Rice Medley (Diane M) .............................................................44

Pasta ...........................................................................................45

Carbonara Pasta (icnmgrjill) ....................................................................45

Macaroni and Cheese (Carole) ..................................................................45

White Cheese Chicken Lasagna (Carole) ........................................................45

Tomatoless Spaghetti (Dawn Grace) ............................................................46

Chicken Spaghetti (Carole) .....................................................................46

Cheesy Bacon, Chicken & Spaghetti Casserole (Carole) ........................................46

Shrimp Pasta in a Cream Sauce (Diane M) ......................................................47

Spinach Fettuccine (Diane M) ..................................................................47

Risotto w/Lobster, Chicken or Shrimp (Diane M) ..............................................47

Garden Primavera Pasta (Diane M) .............................................................47

Linguine with Ricotta, Eggplant & Basil (Diane M) .............................................48

Fettuccine with Zucchini & Mushrooms (Diane M) .............................................48

Fettuccine Alfredo (Diane M) ..................................................................48

Linguine with Clam Sauce (Diane M) ...........................................................48

Vegetables .....................................................................................49

Olive Oil, Garlic & Romano Cheese Mashed Cauliflower (Carole) ..............................49

Roasted Brussel Sprouts (Nekura) ..............................................................49

Cheesy Red Potato & Dill Au Gratin (bbear) ...................................................49

Easy baked Zucchini (Carole) ..................................................................50

Sweet Potato Casserole (Carole) ...............................................................50

Butterscotch Yams (Diane M) ..................................................................50

Sesame Carrots and Cabbage (AgilityMe) .......................................................50

Squash Dressing (Diane M) .....................................................................50

Broccoli with Garlic & Olive Oil (Diane M) ....................................................50

Roasted Garlic (Diane M) ................................................................................................51

Spinach with Parmesan and Almonds (Diane M) ..............................................................51

Roasted Vegetable Calzone (Diane M) ............................................................................51

Stuffed Artichokes (leelee) ............................................................................................51

Sweet Potato Fries (Verdicries) ......................................................................................52

Mushroom Rice Medley (Diane M) ..................................................................................52

## Soups ................................................................................................................53

Simple Chicken Soup (Loveslife) ....................................................................................53

White Bean Chicken Chili (Bladderella) ...........................................................................53

Honey Carrot Soup (Carole) ..........................................................................................54

Best Carrot Soup Ever (Briza) ........................................................................................54

Bacon Cheddar Cauliflower Chowder (Carole) .................................................................54

Beef Leek Barley Stew (RaiinbowEyes) ...........................................................................55

Fiesta Corn Potato Chowder (Raiinboweyes) ...................................................................55

Super Easy DIY Vegetable Broth (Tectonic) .....................................................................56

Asian Mushroom Soup (sandberg4) ................................................................................56

Sweet Potato Pear Soup (Carole) ...................................................................................56

Roasted Eggplant Soup (egrolman) ................................................................................56

Split Pea Soup (agilityme) .............................................................................................57

Chicken Tortellini Soup (Diane M) ...................................................................................57

Avocado Tortilla Soup  (Carole) ......................................................................................57

Gypsy Soup and Molasses Bread (Briza) .........................................................................57

Baked Potato Soup (leelee88) ........................................................................................58

Corn and Cheese Chowder (Carole) ...............................................................................58

## Salads & Salad Dressings ........................................................................................59

### SALADS ...............................................................................................................59

Macaroni Salad with Creamy Dressing (Carole) ...............................................................59

Kale Salad Recipe (Emilywst) .........................................................................................59

Potato Salad with Creamy Dill Dressing (Carole) .............................................................59

Cucumber and Peach Salad (Carole) ..............................................................................60

Sweet Pepper Salad (Carole) .........................................................................................60

Green Bean & Feta Salad (Diane M) ................................................................................60

Pasta Salad with Cucumber Dressing (Carole) .................................................................60

### SALAD DRESSINGS .................................................................................................60

Hummus Salad Dressing (Briza) .....................................................................................60

Chip Dip or Salad Dressing (Jenn) ..................................................................................61

Cheesy Dill Salad Dressing (Carole) ...............................................................................61

Cottage Cheese Salad Dressing (Diane M.) .....................................................................61

Roasted Garlic Olive Oil Dressing (Diane M) ....................................................................61

Root Beer Cream Salad Dressing (Carole) .......................................................................61

Cheese Lovers Salad Dressing (Carole) ............................................................................61

Creamy Dilly Cucumber Dressing (Carole) ..........................................................................61

Mock Red Wine Salad Dressing (Carole) ............................................................................62

Tropical Cream Salad Dressing (Carole) .............................................................................62

Cheesy Garlic Salad Dressing (Carole) ..............................................................................62

## Breads, Muffins & Scones ............................................................................................63

### BREAD ....................................................................................................................63

My Mom's Wonderful English Muffin Bread (Bladderella) .....................................................63

Sausage Asiago Bubble Bread (Carole) .............................................................................63

Pear Bread (Carole) ........................................................................................................64

Old Fashioned Potato Bread (Carole) ................................................................................64

Pear Cardamom Bread (Kelly B) .......................................................................................64

Homemade Cinnamon Bread (Carole) ...............................................................................65

Apple Cinnamon Bread (Carole) .......................................................................................65

Pumpkin Bread (Verdicries) .............................................................................................66

Focaccia Bread (Diane M) ...............................................................................................66

Irish Soda Bread (Diane M) .............................................................................................66

Heavenly Coconut Date Bread (Loveslife) ..........................................................................67

### MUFFINS, BISCUITS & SCONES ................................................................................67

Blueberry Cornbread Muffins (Carole) ...............................................................................67

Oatmeal Muffins (icnmgrjill) ............................................................................................67

Cottage Cheese Biscuits (Carole) .....................................................................................68

Red Lobster Cheddar Bay Biscuits (Carole) ........................................................................68

Bacon Cheese Biscuit (Carole) ........................................................................................68

Blueberry Scones (Hazel) ................................................................................................68

Cheddar Cheese Scones (Carole) .....................................................................................69

Apple Scones (Carole) ....................................................................................................69

## Dessert ...................................................................................................................70

### CAKES & CUPCAKES ...............................................................................................70

Oatmeal Cake (Robin) ....................................................................................................70

Applesauce Cake (Diane M) ............................................................................................70

Fluffy Yellow Cupcakes (Bladderella) ................................................................................70

Banana Cupcakes with Peanut Butter Frosting (Carole) .......................................................71

Pecan Pie cupcakes (Carole) ...........................................................................................72

Peach Cupcakes with Peach Buttercream Frosting (Carole) ..................................................72

Blueberry Crumb Cake (Carole) .......................................................................................72

Italian Cream Cake (Carole) ............................................................................................73

Tres Leches Cake (Carole) ..............................................................................................73

Sweet Potato Cheesecake (Carole) ...................................................................................74

White Chocolate Banana Cake (carole) ..............................................................................74

Coconut Peach Cake (Carole)...........................................................................74

Carrot Cake (Carole).........................................................................................75

White Chocolate Pound Cake (Diane M)...........................................................75

PIE..........................................................................................................................75

Caramel Pie (Carole)........................................................................................75

Oatmeal Pie (Carole)........................................................................................76

Easy Pumpkin Pie Ice Cream or Ice Cream Pie (wheresmysmokes)...............76

Eggnog Pumpkin Pie (Carole)...........................................................................76

Angel Food Pie (Diane M).................................................................................76

Frozen Blueberry Cream Sandwiches (Blazer)..................................................77

Fruit Cobbler (Diane M).....................................................................................77

Baked Indian Pudding (Diane M)......................................................................77

Fried Coconut Puffs (Carole)............................................................................77

Mint White Chocolate Mousse (Carole)............................................................77

Coffee Break Treat (Blazer)..............................................................................78

COOKIES.................................................................................................................78

Cashew Butter Cookies (Clevsea).....................................................................78

Snowball Cookies (wcrox).................................................................................78

Carob Brownies (emilyandlouise)......................................................................78

Butterscotch Brownies (Diane M).....................................................................79

Crunchy Cookies (Diane M)..............................................................................79

Peanut Butter Cookies Gluten Free (agilityme).................................................79

Pear Custard Bars (Diane M)............................................................................79

Cake Batter Fudge (Carole)..............................................................................80

Appendix A. ...............................................................................................................81

2012 ICN Food List...............................................................................................81

Appendix B .................................................................................................................92

What You Should Know About Food & Pesticides.................................................92

The Dirty Dozen™ 2015...................................................................................92

The Clean Fifteen™..........................................................................................93

Appendix C .................................................................................................................94

Frequently Asked Questions .................................................................................94

"What if foods don't bother my bladder?".........................................................94

"Should I buy organic fruits and veggies?".......................................................94

"How much water should I drink?"....................................................................94

"I'm afraid to eat anything. What should I do?".................................................94

"I react to some foods on the Bladder Friendly/Safe list. Why?" .....................94

"Why can I eat a food one day and, a few days later, flare from it?"................95

"Why does my food tolerance vary with my menstrual cycle?" ........................95

"I feel like I react to every food. What should I do?" .......................................95

"I can't live without my soda. What should I do?" .................................................................95

"Coffee in the morning helps me have a bowel movement. What should I do?" ...........95

"I've lived on junk food. It's what I've always eaten but now it hurts. What can I do?" ........96

"I'm not a cook. I don't really know how to cook, what should I do?" ...............................96

"Some acidic foods, like lemon, become alkaline in the body. Shouldn't I eat these?" ........96

"Should I drink alkaline water?" ..............................................................................96

"Is juicing safe for IC?" .........................................................................................96

**Appendix D** ..........................................................................................................**97**

More Books on the IC Diet ......................................................................................97

A Taste of the Good Life: A Cookbook for an IC Diet ...............................................97

Confident Choices: Customizing the IC Diet .........................................................97

Confident Choices: A Cookbook for IC & OAB .......................................................97

Confident Choices: A Guide For Nutrition Educators .............................................97

The Happy Bladder Cookbook .............................................................................97

The Happy Bladder Christmas Cookbook .............................................................98

IC Friendly Fit & Fresh ........................................................................................98

**Appendix E** ..........................................................................................................**99**

Fighting Constipation With Fiber ...........................................................................99

**Appendix F** ........................................................................................................**101**

Fatigue Fighting Foods .........................................................................................101

Water ...............................................................................................................101

Eggs ................................................................................................................101

Whole Grains ....................................................................................................101

Blueberries .......................................................................................................101

Almonds ...........................................................................................................101

Popcorn ............................................................................................................101

Broccoli & Spinach .............................................................................................102

Sweet Potatoes .................................................................................................102

Salmon .............................................................................................................102

Grass Fed Beef .................................................................................................102

Low Acid Coffee ................................................................................................102

**Appendix G** .......................................................................................................**102**

Five-Step Coffee Challenge ...................................................................................102

About Interstitial Cystitis .......................................................................................103

About the IC Network ............................................................................................103

IC Chef Cookbook History .....................................................................................105

# Introduction

By Jill Heidi Osborne MA, Founder of the IC Network

Most patients with interstitial cystitis and/or chronic prostatitis quickly learn that certain foods exacerbate their symptoms, including foods high in acid (i.e. coffee, tea, soda, lemon, cranberry, etc.), foods that stimulate nerves (caffeine) and/or foods that contain substances that promote inflammation (i.e. histamine, chocolate, alcohols). Despite multiple research studies that have proven the irritating effects of these foods, some medical care providers still tell patients that diet modification isn't necessary or important.

Patients, too, often underestimate the importance of diet modification. Consider Judy, an IC patient in New York. Shortly after her diagnosis, she called the IC Network for information. It was a long, memorable conversation during which I explained key facts about IC and diet. I heard from her again five years later when she called sobbing in pain. As we talked, it was clear that her symptoms were consistent with bladder wall irritation. She had pain and discomfort as her bladder filled with urine that was relieved after urination.

I asked, *"Are you following the IC Diet?"* She loudly said, *"Yes."* Her husband said, *"No, she's never followed the diet. She drinks a pot of coffee a day followed by a six pack of diet coke."* She cried out, *"That's right. Take away everything I love."* I was astonished.

So I asked, *"Didn't you believe me when I told you about the diet?* She said *"No."* I responded, *"But didn't you believe Dr. Robert Moldwin when he told you about the diet?"* She said, *"No. I didn't think it applied to me."* This was the mindset of a woman terribly addicted to coffee, caffeine and soda. She failed to grasp the key concept that acid poured on a wound every day can prevent healing and cause more pain and discomfort. Three months after starting the diet, she called me back and shared that her symptoms had improved dramatically.

The IC diet focuses on the use of fresh meats, fruits and veggies that you prepare at home so that you know exactly what they contain. The challenge, of course, is the prevalence of fast food and manufactured foods in our daily lives that are chock of fill of an amazing array of additives and chemicals. We know, for example, that foods containing sugar and high fructose corn syrup trigger addiction and are the leading contributor of rising obesity around the world. This is a deliberate attempt on the part of those manufacturers to create a recurring customer base. Many artificial sweeteners (i.e. aspartame, NutraSweet®), preservatives, food colorings, flavorings (i.e. citric acid, etc.) and flavor enhancers (i.e. monosodium glutamate, etc.) can also trigger bladder symptoms. When IC strikes, it's time to get back to simple, fresh & healthy food.

Whether you're newly diagnosed or a veteran IC patient, this cookbook offers recipes developed, adapted and/or tested by other IC patients. Of course, not every recipe will work for every patient because we often have very individual food sensitivities. But, it's a place to start and, I hope, rediscover the joys of fresh, healthy food.

The proceeds of book sales will be used to underwrite the Interstitial Cystitis Network patient education and support activities, including the annual IC Awareness Month campaign.

## How Foods & Chemicals Irritate The Bladder?

The purpose of the bladder is to contain the toxic, irritating chemicals found in urine. It does so by having a very thick layer of mucus, known as the GAG or glycosaminoglycan layer, which keeps urine away from the more fragile cells of the bladder wall. When the bladder wall (aka urothelium) and GAG layer are damaged, urea, ammonia and other toxins penetrate deeply into the tissue where they cause profound irritation, inflammation and the classic symptoms of IC. The hallmark symptom of bladder wall damage is an increase in symptoms, discomfort and/or pain as the bladder fills with urine that is relieved after urination.

A note to smokers. Did you know that many of the thousands of chemicals produced by cigarettes are processed through the kidneys and end up in the urine? Those chemicals saturate the bladder wall and, over time, can trigger the development of bladder cancer. In fact, smoking is the #1 risk factor for bladder cancer. But, if you have a damaged bladder wall and continue to smoke, you're introducing proven carcinogens more deeply into your bladder tissue. If you think IC is bad, bladder cancer is much worse and can be fatal. It's very important that you give up smoking immediately.

## Ingredients Which Often Cause Problems

So, you ask, which are the foods or ingredients that cause the most problems? Here are the top offenders!

**CAFFEINE** - In healthy men and women, caffeine triggers bladder symptoms. Researchers in Massachusetts found that healthy men who drank an average of 2 cups of coffee per day were more likely to develop lower urinary tract symptoms and difficulty with urine storage while healthy women developed progressively worse symptoms of urgency. (Intake of caffeinated, carbonated, or citrus beverage types and development of lower urinary tract symptoms in men and women.) Caffeine acts as a diuretic, stimulating more frequent urination and also causes urine to become more concentrated with urea and ammonia. In the IC patient, these effects are magnified. All caffeinated products (coffees, teas, green teas, energy drinks, sodas, etc.) should be stopped immediately.

**ACIDIC FOODS** - Foods high in acid (i.e. citrus fruits and juices, cranberry, vinegar) create irritation in much the same way that acid poured on a wound on your hand would feel. It hurts! Cranberries, for example, contain quinic, malic and citric acid, which explains why cranberry juice is irritating for most of us. All citrus fruits and juices should be stopped immediately, as well as concentrated tomato products (i.e. tomato sauce, paste, etc.)

**ALCOHOL** – Just as alcohol sprayed on a wound hurts, alcohol which enters a damaged bladder wall triggers irritation and pain. In an ICN Survey, beer, wine and spirits bothered roughly 95% patients though there is some wiggle room with lower acid varieties. Clear pale ales were better tolerated than darker porters and brown ales. Lower acid wines were more bladder friendly than high acid wines. Surprisingly, clear spirits (i.e. sake, vodka) were found to be the most bladder friendly of all, usually because they are combined with bladder friendly mixers such as ice, water, or milk.

**POTASSIUM** – Some, but not all, patients report that foods high in potassium have triggered bladder discomfort though the IC diet research studies have found that bananas and yams, both high in potassium, are usually bladder soothing. Try small amounts of high potassium foods to see if you tolerate them well.

**HISTAMINE** - Researchers have found that some IC patients have high numbers of activated mast cells in their bladder wall. These mast cells release histamine, which then triggers frequency, urgency and/or pain. Not surprisingly, foods rich in histamine (i.e. red wine, anchovies, ciders, sauerkraut, smoked fish, sour cream, etc.) or cause the release of histamine may trigger bladder and/or bowel discomfort in some, but not all patients.

**ARTIFICIAL SWEETENERS** – Research studies and patient stories have confirmed that many artificial sweeteners (aspartame, saccharin, sucralose, etc.) appear to be bladder irritating, particularly aspartame (i.e. NutraSweet®). Most "diet" products, such as sugar free iced tea or soda, should be avoided.

2

**MSG, NITRITES & NITRATES** - MSG is a mast cell degranulator and for patients sensitive or allergic to it, can cause rash, hives, asthma and sudden diarrhea known as "Chinese Restaurant Syndrome." We suggest purchasing low salt soups and broths, which generally do not include MSG (i.e. Campbell's Health Request® soups). IC patients have long reported that foods containing high levels of nitrites and nitrates (i.e. deli meats, preserved meats, processed foods, etc.) can also trigger bladder symptoms. Look for nitrate free, uncured bacon and sausage products instead. These are generally better tolerated and, frankly, taste better too!

**MULTIVITAMINS** – Both patients and research studies report that multivitamins can trigger bladder symptoms due to high levels of Vitamin C (ascorbic acid). The best source of vitamins is from fresh fruits and vegetables. Vitamin C, for example, is found in green, yellow or red bell peppers, leafy greens, broccoli, peas and papayas that are generally well tolerated in the sensitive bladder. Citrus sources for Vitamin C should be avoided. Vitamin B6 may also be irritating for some patients when taken in supplement form. Foods rich in vitamin B6, however, are generally safe, including: fresh meats, fish, poultry, organ meats, nuts, lentils, potatoes, carrot juice, avocado and prunes. If you need a multivitamin, try **MultiRight®** (www.multiright.com), a low acid multivitamin and mineral complex that the IC Network helped to develop. It works well for many patients.

**SUPPLEMENTS** - Many patients desperate for relief visit their local vitamin store in search of products that can help. Rarely do the employees know the difference between interstitial cystitis and bacterial cystitis, often recommending cranberry based products. Some also suggest that harsh "cleansing protocols" should be done under the mistaken assumption that bacteria are present. IC patients do not have infection and these protocols are generally much too harsh for our tender bladders and bowels. However, there are some supplements that were designed to encourage bladder health and healing and/or have been studied with interstitial cystitis patients. These include: CystoProtek®, CystaQ®, Desert Harvest Ale® and, most recently, a new product called Cysto Renew®.

**CHOCOLATE** – Chocolate contains several ingredients that have the potential to exacerbate IC symptoms: theobromine, caffeine, phenylethylamine, tannins and oxalates. Well known for triggering migraine headaches, IC patients often report flares from eating chocolates, particularly cheaper milk chocolate products. White chocolate and carob, however, are more bladder friendly. Expensive dark chocolates, too, may be more bladder tolerable for some, but not all, patients.

## The IC Food Lists

In the past twenty years, many food lists have emerged for interstitial cystitis. Some were created by patients while others were developed by doctors or pharmaceutical companies. The most credible early list was created by Bev Laumann, former Orange County CA IC Support group leader and author of **A Taste of the Good Life: A Cookbook for an IC Diet**. Alza Pharmaceuticals and, later, Ortho Urology launched the "IC Smart Diet", a one-page tear off sheet that doctors gave out. Unfortunately, it contained a glaring error by stating that eggs should be avoided. Eggs are, in fact, a cornerstone breakfast foods for patients with a sensitive bladder.

IC patient Julie Beyer RD sought to educate other dietitians about the role of foods in IC and to share the IC food list. She was met with a common critique *"Where's the research proving that diet matters in IC?"* Thankfully, IC patient Barbara Shorter RD, PhD conducted those groundbreaking studies with Dr. Robert Moldwin (author of the **Interstitial Cystitis Survival Guide**) at Long Island University. Today, we have great clarity on the foods that can trigger bladder and prostate discomfort.

Most patients start with the Long Island University (LIU) Food Lists, which identify the most common irritating foods. This is the perfect place for patients to begin by eliminating the high-risk foods like coffee's, teas, alcohols, citrus fruits and so forth. But it also identifies foods that cause the least bother. So, if you're trying to figure out what to eat, the least bothersome foods are a great place to begin with, of course, some common sense. We certainly don't want you to put hot sauce on a steak, lemon juice in water and so forth. This list, however, should not be interpreted as the only foods an IC patient can eat. There are many more that can work as well. Please refer to the ICN Food List for a much broader list of foods.

| The Most Bothersome Foods | The Least Bothersome Foods |
| --- | --- |
| **Coffee** – regular & decaf | **Water** |
| **Tea** – caffeinated | **Milk** – low-fat & whole |
| **Carbonated beverages** – cola, non-colas, diet & caffeine-free | **Fruits** – bananas, blueberries, honeydew melon, pears, raisins, watermelon |
| **Alcohols** – beer, red wine, white wine, champagne | **Vegetables** – broccoli, brussel sprouts, cabbage, carrots, cauliflower, celery, cucumber, |
| **Fruits** – grapefruit, lemon, orange, pineapple | mushrooms, peas, radishes, squash, zucchini, |
| **Fruit Juice** – cranberry, grapefruit, orange, pineapple | white potatoes, sweet potatoes & yams |
| **Vegetables** – tomato & tomato products | **Poultry** - chicken, eggs, turkey, |
| **Flavor Enhancers** – hot peppers, spicy foods, chili, horseradish, vinegar, monosodium glutamate (MSG) | **Meat** – beef, pork, lamb |
| **Artificial Sweeteners** – NutraSweet™, Sweet 'N Low®, Equal®, saccharin | **Seafood** – shrimp, tuna fish, salmon |
| **Ethnic foods** – Mexican, Thai, Indian | **Grains** - oat, rice |
| | **Snacks** – pretzels, popcorn |

The more comprehensive ICN Food List was created to help patients add diversity to their diet. Created with the help of Bev Laumann (author of **A Taste of the Good Life: A Cookbook for an IC Diet**), Julie Beyer RD (author of the **Confident Choices: Customizing the IC Diet, Confident Choices: A Cookbook for IC & OAB & Interstitial Cystitis: A Nutrition Guide For Educators**), Barbara Shorter RD PhD (author of numerous IC diet research studies) and Barbara Gordon RD (former ICA executive director), it rates more than 300 foods in three categories "Bladder Friendly", "Try It" & "Caution." Patients generally start with the foods in the bladder friendly category and then, as their symptoms improve, slowly add foods in the try it column. Foods in the Caution category are rarely eaten. The latest revision, our 2012 list, can be found in Appendix A or can be downloaded from the IC Network website. The next revision will occur in 2016.

## About The Recipes

The recipes and suggestions in this cookbook are very diverse. Some were adapted from other recipes to make them more bladder friendly while others are entirely the creation of the patient who submitted. You'll find both simple and complex recipes. Some are very bladder friendly while others might contain some risk foods that could flare you. Your job is to pick and choose based upon your own unique dietary sensitivities. If a recipe contains something that you know has caused flares, either remove that ingredient or substitute it with a more bladder friendly option (see next section). Our goal is to give you some fun, new recipes to try and/or experiment with.

## Abbreviations & Substitutions

tsp = teaspoon
tbsp = tablespoon
oz = ounce
lb = pound

**Canned Soup** - Use a low salt, MSG free soup

**Lemon Flavor** - lemon peel or zest

**Lemon Juice** - pear juice instead

**Vinegar** - pear or blueberry juice

**Red Wine** – blueberry juice

**White Wine** – pear juice

**Low Acid Coffees** – Simpatico®, Puroast®    *Lucy Joe's brand*

**Herbal Coffees** – Pero®, Cafix®, Kaffree Roma®, Teeccino®

**Apples** - Gala and Fuji apples are considered the lowest in acid.

**Milk Chocolate** – white chocolate, carob

**Ice Cream** - Look for brands that use real cream, milk and sugar. Vanilla preferred. Avoid irritating flavors like chocolate or citrus.

**Cake Mixes** - organic baking mixes such as European Gourmet®, Bob's Red Mill®

**Artificial Sweeteners** – Splenda® appears to be more bladder friendly than most other artificial sweeteners BUT we believe more research is necessary to prove that they are safe for long term consumption. Try to minimize the use of all sweetening products, as well as high fructose corn syrup and traditional sugar products to avoid developing a sugar or "sweet" addiction.

**Pickles** – Bubbies Kosher Dill Pickles are made without vinegar and may provide a sour flavor without the extra acid!

**Onions** – Try chives

# Beverages

## HOT DRINKS

### White Chocolate Vanilla Bean "Cocoa" w/ Cinnamon Whipped Cream (n2indigoky)

3 cups whole milk
1 cup of good quality white chocolate chopped
1 vanilla bean (*I use a Madagascar vanilla bean*)
sugar or honey to taste
1 cup whipping cream
dash cinnamon

Put milk in saucepan and split vanilla bean scrape out the middle and add the whole bean and scrapings to the milk (and or brewed coffee) slowly bring to a boil add white chocolate and then top with fresh whipped cream with a dash of cinnamon. Enjoy! It's my Sunday morning splurge!

*\* You can also use no acid coffee to make this a latte, which is delicious! Add one cup of coffee in lieu of one of the cups of milk.*

### Karen's Vanilla Steamer (kagey)

½ cup cold milk
vanilla or almond syrup
whipping cream/cinnamon for topping

Blend the milk briskly using a handheld, electric or battery-operated frother. This is called stretching the milk. Then add vanilla or almond syrup to taste. I use Flavorganics® French vanilla or almond syrup. You can use Starbucks Vanilla Syrup or a carob flavoring too. After frothing, stick into microwave and heat for a hot drink on a cold morning. Top with whipping cream and cinnamon if desired. It's also good cold. There are so many things you can do with this simple recipe.

### Karen's Hot Drink Topping (kagey)

2 cups heavy whipping cream
honey to taste

Beat whipping cream with an electric mixer in a deep bowl on high until peaks form. Add honey to taste, beat together. Scoop on top of your hot drink. Sprinkle with cinnamon if desired. Add some sliced almonds on top. Enjoy!

### Vanilla Herbal Coffee (lizzylu)

Heat up vanilla almond milk and a tsp. of Kaffree Roma® and voila. It's like having a vanilla coffee (well, sort of) but it's really good.

### Hot Butterscotch (GayleK)

4 cups (1 qt.) milk
1 cup (6 oz.) butterscotch chips
½ cup miniature marshmallows

In a medium saucepan, combine all ingredients over medium heat. Whisk until chips and marshmallows are melted and mixture is heated through. Serve immediately.

### Steamed Almond Milk with Carob (jwlrs)

Add 1 tsp. carob powder to 1 cup almond milk. Steam it. Yum!

## White Hot Chocolate (percy)

*This drink is very IC friendly though not diet friendly.*

1 cup whole milk
1 cup half and half
¼ lb. white chocolate *(chopped or chips)*
½ tsp. vanilla
peppermint sticks

Heat milk and half and half on medium just below a simmer. Remove pot from heat and add the white chocolate. When the chocolate has melted, add the vanilla and stir. Reheat very gently. Serve with a peppermint stick as a stirrer.

## White Peppermint Hot Chocolate (Carole)

8 oz. white chocolate, chopped
3 ½ cups milk
6 hard peppermint candies, crushed fine
½ tsp. peppermint extract
⅔ cup whipping cream

Beat chilled cream with crushed mints until stiff peaks form. Refrigerate for about an hour. Meanwhile, heat milk to a simmer then mix in chocolate. Whisk until chocolate is melted and smooth. Add mint extract and stir through. Pour into mugs and top with minty whipped cream.

## White Peppermint Patty (Soupey28)

*This delicious holiday drink is something that you can drink all year long! I love white chocolate and it's a great alternative to cocoa (plus the peppermint relaxes my bladder and maybe that can help you)!*

1 oz. white chocolate (or chocolate alternative)
¼ tsp. peppermint extract
8 oz. milk
2 tsp. white sugar

Heat milk to a simmer then mix in sugar, peppermint extract and chocolate until melted. If you decide to serve for guests you can always add in a peppermint or cinnamon stick for flavor and decoration.

## Delicious Hot Caramel (ktmeak7)

I just heat a mug of milk in my microwave for one minute and ten seconds. Add 1 tbsp. of Smucker's caramel sundae syrup. Stir and enjoy!

## Hot White Chocolate (Diane M)

1 cup heavy cream
6 oz. white chocolate, cut into small pieces
3 cup milk
½ tsp. vanilla extract

Cook heavy cream in small saucepan over med/low heat. Place chocolate in heat proof bowl and set aside. When cream simmers (about 4 min), remove from heat and pour over chocolate. When chocolate begins to melt, stir to combine cream and chocolate until mixture is melted. Set aside.

In a saucepan over medium heat, warm milk until hot but not boiling (about five minutes). When milk steams, reduce heat and slowly whisk in chocolate mixture until combined. Remove from heat and whisk in vanilla. Whisk until light foam forms. Ladle into heat proof bowls and serve immediately.

## Honey Tea (fmcbride)

*Since we are so limited with drinks friendly to IC I have found I enjoy a tea with honey.*

1 generous spoon of Sue Bee® spun honey
1 cup very hot (boiling) water.

## Hot Milk with Maple Syrup (DawnGrace)

Microwave a cup of milk of your choice. Add maple syrup to your liking and stir. Serve hot on a cold day.

## Starlight Mint (DawnGrace)

Crack up some Starlight Peppermint candy and put in a baggie. Keep in your purse or desk at work. Heat one cup of water in microwave. Stir in a few pieces of cracked Starlight Mints till dissolved. Makes a wonderful hot drink. You can have one in a restaurant if you want anytime, just have them bring the hot water.

## My Favorite Pumpkin Pie Latte (Daisy)

1-2 tbsp. canned pumpkin
2 tbsp. vanilla extract
¼ tsp. cinnamon
¼ tsp. ginger
1 cup soymilk
1 tbsp. Silk® creamer, optional
3 tsp. honey, sugar or sweetener to taste
½ cup strong low acid coffee or herbal coffee substitute

In a saucepan, heat soymilk, Silk® creamer, sugar and pumpkin puree until steaming. Stir in vanilla, cinnamon and ginger. Remove from heat. Blend with a hand blender until thick and foamy. Pour into a large mug, along with the brewed coffee. Top with a sprinkling of ground nutmeg.

## Hot Pumpkin Pie Milk Drink (icyjunomary)

4 cups 1% organic milk
½ cup canned organic pumpkin
¼ cup or less organic sugar - to taste
½ tsp. cinnamon
½ tsp. ginger
¼ tsp. nutmeg
¼ tsp. cloves

Mix all together in a blender and then pour the amount that you want hot (say one cup) into a saucepan and heat and stir until it is hot. Microwaving makes it foam up and all over your microwave!!! Store the unused portion in the refrigerator. Omit any of the spices that bother your IC. Add a dollop of low fat whipped cream if you like and it will taste like you are having pumpkin pie to drink. I like this cold as well. Enjoy!

## Dulce De Leche (Angeles)

Dulce de Leche was originated in Argentina and it is used in cakes, croissants, crepes, ice cream or simply as a spread on French bread over butter for breakfast. That's how I used to eat it as a child. Dulce de Leche is available in the US under Milk Caramel or Caramel Milk. In some places you can find it as Dulce de Leche.

Dulce de Leche is basically milk and sugar cooked slowly until it gets a creamy consistency and brown color. For a warm drink, I warmed milk (hot) and added 2 spoons of Dulce de Leche and stirred it, you can also put it in the blender if it doesn't dissolve well. It is delicious!

## Peanutbuttery Butterscotch Dream (OllieR)

¾ mug worth of milk
1 rounded tbsp. of peanut butter
20-30 butterscotch morsels to taste
mini marshmallows

Measure out the mug of milk and pour it in a saucepan to heat on medium-high. While the milk is warming, heat the butterscotch morsels in a small microwave safe bowl on high for about 25 seconds. Take out and combine it with the peanut butter. Stick the whole mixture back in the microwave for 20-25 more seconds until very melted and nearly runny. Pour the mixture in the bottom of the mug, pouring the heated milk on top when it is ready. Mix well. It will take a little bit for it to all dissolve together. Top with mini marshmallows.

## Coconut Cream Caramel (Carole)

½ cup organic coconut milk
½ cup milk
2 tbsp. caramel syrup or more to taste (I use Smuckers® syrup)

Heat above ingredients to boiling. Garnish with fresh whipped cream, shredded coconut and drizzle syrup on top.

## Pear Cider for the Sweet Tooth in You! (OllieR)

*I hate pear juice cold, but warm it with spices and it tastes quite delicious! This is a recipe for a sweeter tasting cider, perfect for dessert or a morning treat.*

For a single mug of pear cider:
1 mug worth of pear juice (RW Knudsen®)
½ tbsp. cinnamon
½ tbsp. ginger
½ tbsp. allspice

dash of nutmeg
1-2 tbsp. white sugar*

If you like more flavor you can add a little more of each ingredient. Pour the pear juice into a saucepan and heat it to a little less than boiling. Add in the cinnamon, ginger, allspice, and nutmeg and stir. When the beverage is nice and hot stir in the white sugar until it dissolves. I do not dilute the pear juice and it does not bother my IC however the kind I buy is already diluted with water.

*I buy pear juice with no sugar added and it needs an extra bit when I make the cider, but if you buy one with extra sugar or one that is less diluted you may not need this.

## Eggnog Latte (LovesLife)

*I've already taken my favorite eggnog and just warmed it up which is quite yum but then decided to make a latte with it using my coffee substitute. It is decadent. Of course, you'll need to find an eggnog that you can tolerate or make your own. Fortunately for me, I've done okay with Trader Joes eggnog. There's also other organic nogs that have even less stuff in them but I guess it just comes down to knowing what you can tolerate.*

½ cup of eggnog, warmed up in a pan
1 cup of strong Teeccino® or other coffee substitute
1 tsp. sugar or to taste
pinch of nutmeg
dollop of whip cream

Beat the eggnog with a mini blender. Pour the coffee in your mug, add the eggnog, stir in sugar, add the dollop of whip cream and sprinkle on the nutmeg and enjoy!

## Chocolate Coconut Cream (Carole)

½ cup organic coconut milk
½ cup milk
2 tbsp. powdered white hot chocolate mix

Mix and heat to boiling above ingredients. Garnish with cinnamon and shaved white chocolate. UMMM very yummy!

## Mexican Hot "Carob-cocoa" (loveslife)

*I've always loved Mexican hot chocolate but obviously can't have it now. So I came up with this alternative that is incredibly close for me to feel pretty happy with a mug in front of me! I think the carob has enough bitterness of true cocoa and the white chocolate obviously balances out the flavor with its cocoa butter. What's really nifty is that I'll zip up the portions in a zip lock back and when I'm at my fave coffee house, I'll have them throw it in my mug and give me a hot steamed milk and I can hang with the crowd!*

2 cups whole milk
2 tbsp. carob powder
4 tbsp. white chocolate chips (*try to find ones that actually contain cocoa butter without junk. Trader Joe's has some great ones right now*)
¼ tsp. cinnamon (*if can tolerate*)

Put all in a pot and bring to a low simmer, stirring to melt the white chocolate and blend the ingredients. Pour into your favorite mug and enjoy!

## Mocha Free Mocha Latte (loveslife)

8 oz. of strong Teeccino® Maya Caffe herbal coffee (I use 2 scoops in my small French press)
1 tbsp. carob powder
8 oz. whole milk
1 tsp. vanilla
1-2 tbsp. raw sugar

Put the carob powder, vanilla and sugar to taste in a tall mug. Pour in the hot Teeccino®. Stir to blend. Microwave milk for 2 to 3 minutes until very hot in a large Pyrex measuring cup. Put a wire whip into the cup and spin it between your hands (as if you're rubbing your hands together) until your milk gets real foamy. Pour most of this on top of your coffee mix. Stir to blend. Top with remaining foam.

## Yummy Hot Carob Drink (Marmotte)

Liquefy:
½ cup raw, unsalted cashews or blanched slivered almonds

½ cup water
2 tbsp. carob powder
¼ tsp. salt
1 tsp. vanilla
1 tbsp. sweetener (or to taste)
½ tsp. Inka or other coffee substitute

Add:
2 ½ cups water

Heat for a hot drink, or refrigerate for cold carob milk. It's delicious either way.

## Carob Mocha Powdered Mix (Marmotte)

*Since everyone in our family love this, I make it up as a powder to have on hand. Just add to hot water and go.*

1 cup carob powder
2 tsp. salt
1 ½ cup sugar cane crystals
2 tbsp. Inka, Pero® or other coffee substitute
6 cups milk powder (your choice of brand)

Mix thoroughly and store in airtight container. Add 4-5 T. to a mug of hot water. Stir and enjoy.

## Peppermint & Chamomile Tea with Honey (flowergirl)

I mix peppermint tea and chamomile with honey. It tastes great and it makes my bladder feel great.

## Karen's Hot Cinnamon Tea (kagey)

*(Only for patients who can tolerate cinnamon)*

2 quarts water
2 or 3 cinnamon sticks
1-2 tsp. ground cinnamon

Heat 2 quarts water in microwave to boiling. Drop cinnamon sticks in water and let steep. Add 1 or 2 tsp. of ground cinnamon. Use a quality cinnamon from Saigon or Vietnam. It tends to have a sweetness to it. Enjoy!!

## Caffixiccino Recipe (beverlyann)

2 tbsp. Cafix® *(substituting NOT recommended)*
12 oz. of plain coconut milk beverage or almond milk beverage *(both in the dairy case)*
10 drops toffee flavored Stevia
Dash of fresh ground Ceylon true cinnamon
Dash of fresh ground nutmeg *(optional)*

Place all ingredients in a pot and bring to a near boil. To form a frothy top, blend with a stick blender. Pour, drink and enjoy. For a cool summer treat, blend in a blender with a little ice.

# SHAKES & CREAMY DRINKS

## Homemade Almond Milk (Briza)

2 cups almonds
4 cups water
1 tsp. vanilla *(optional)*

Soak almonds overnight. Discard soaking water and rinse almonds in a deep bowl of water. Repeat until water is clear. Place soaked almonds, vanilla, and four cups of water in blender. Blend on highest speed for 2 minutes. Strain milk through cheesecloth or a fine mesh paint strainer bag, discarding solids.

## Eggnog (Carole)

1 egg
2 tbsp. sugar
pinch of salt
1 cup milk
½ tsp. vanilla
sprinkle of nutmeg *(if can tolerate)*

Mix in blender and pour into glass. Enjoy!

## Homemade Shamrock Shake (Jennybird)

*Remember those Shamrock shakes McDonald's used to have in the 80's? Well, I had been thinking about those so I decided to try and make my own.*

Blend:
2 cups peppermint ice cream
Add milk until proper milkshake consistency
1 tsp. vanilla extract
green food coloring *(optional)*

*If you don't have the peppermint stick ice cream. Grind up a few peppermint candies or candy canes in the bottom of your blender. Then add vanilla ice cream. Do not add the vanilla.*

## Blueberry Cobbler (Carole)

8 oz. filtered water
4 oz. blueberry or pomegranate juice (*if can tolerate*)
¼ cup blueberries
1 cup vanilla frozen yogurt (*if can tolerate*)
2 tbsp. honey
1 graham cracker square
dash of cinnamon (*if can tolerate*)
1 cup ice

Blend above ingredients in a blender until smooth.

## Healthier Alternative to Milkshakes (Kadi)

*I love vanilla milkshakes but am really struggling with weight gain due to my IC and Elavil. I came up with this today & it's really good!*

⅔ cup nonfat milk
½ Hadley date almond roll (if you can't find these, it's just a large date with a few chopped almonds)
2 drops of vanilla extract
4 or 5 ice cubes
(I also added a tsp. of Metamucil® Clear & Natural to help with constipation)

I blended it in my Nutribullet but any food processor or blender should work. If you use a regular blender, you might chop up the dates & almonds first into tiny pieces. A vanilla milkshake at InNOut Burger is 16 Weight Watcher® Points Plus. This came out to 3 points. Big difference with way less artery clogging fat.

## Candy Cane Drink (Carole)

1 cup vanilla ice cream
½ cup milk
5-6 drops peppermint extract
3-4 ice cubes
grenadine (*if can tolerate*)
whipping cream
crushed candy cane
candy cane

Place the first four ingredients in a blender and blend. If you can tolerate a little grenadine pour some on the bottom of a glass. Pour ice cream mixture on top. Top with whipped cream and crushed candy cane. Use a candy cane as a stir stick.

*Grenadine may not be tolerated by all ICer's. Please use with caution. Taste is fine without it. It just makes it look more like a candy cane.*

## Protein Shake (Barbm)

Mix 8 oz. of almond milk or vanilla almond mild with one scoop of Jarrow Formulas® unflavored whey protein. It has no artificial sweeteners, flavors, no wheat, gluten or egg. Mix in a blender. 18 grams of protein and total 154 calories! Delicious!

## Coconut Pear Shake (Jinny Jean)

I came up with this recipe a few days ago and even though it is super simple, it is amazing! I take three ripe pears and cut them up and one can of organic coconut milk (with just coconut milk and water) and blend them together. I add about half a cup of water to it as well just to make it a little easier to drink!

## Coconut Milk Shake (Carole)

½ cup coconut
1 cup milk
¼ cup sugar
1 tsp. vanilla extract
2 tbsp. cream (*optional*)

Put all of the ingredients into the blender and mix until smooth.

## CaroNut Shake (OllieR)

*I have a sweet tooth so this recipe has a lot of sugar that can easily be reduced for people reducing their sugar intake. A sugar substitute could work too.*

handful of ice cubes (4 or 5)
6 scoops of vanilla ice cream
6 tbsp. of carob powder
4 tbsp. of brown sugar
2 tbsp. of sugar

2 rounded tsp. crunchy peanut butter
¼ tsp. of almond extract
1/8 tsp. of cinnamon

Put the ice cubes in the blender first to break them up. Then add in all other ingredients and beat it on a high setting. I used liquefy, but you can choose whichever setting is your personal preference for a milk shake consistency. Since having IC, this is the first non-chocolate thing that tasted most like chocolate like me. So if you miss a good old chocolate milk shake you will probably like this one!

*I garnished it with mint for presentation, but this is completely up to you. I actually did not like the mint flavor with it so if you use it as garnish make sure it doesn't get too mixed up into the drink.*

## Blueberry Milk Shake (lizzylu)

*I made myself a blueberry milkshake last weekend and it was delicious and refreshing.*

3 large scoops of vanilla ice cream
a handful of fresh or frozen blueberries
almond milk or regular milk *(the amount depends on the thickness you desire)*
ice *(optional)*

Blend until preferred thickness. Top with whipped cream. This is very important.

# ICED & SWEET TEAS

## Chamomile Honey-Vanilla Iced Tea (Lizzylu)

*I made this over the weekend. It was so hot out and I wanted something refreshing and cool other than water. This did the trick.*

Fill teapot with water and bring to a boil *(does not need to be totally full)*
Add 3 or 4 bags of Chamomile tea
Let steep for a few minutes
Take the tea bags out

While still hot, add 2 tsp. of vanilla extract (without alcohol). I get it from Trader Joe's.
Add a few squeezes of honey. Mix and let cool.
Pour into a pitcher and put in fridge.

## Sweet Mint & Basil Iced Tea (lisa7688)

*A friend of mine made this. I don't know where she got the recipe. The mint and basil seem like an unusual mix but actually blend well together. You could also just make mint iced tea using your own recipe and throw in the basil for something different.*

Half a bunch of fresh mint (about 1 oz.)
Half a bunch of fresh basil (about ½ oz.)
¼ cup honey
8 cups water (½ gallon)

Pour four cups of boiling water over the herbs and let them steep for about 10 minutes. Strain the tea, boil the other four cups of water and steep the leaves again. Mix all of the tea and honey together in a large pitcher. Taste test it. If it's too strong, add a little water to your liking. Refrigerate for at least two hours before serving.

## Mint Ice Tea (Shawnster)

I absolutely miss drinking iced tea in the summer living in Virginia. What I've found to work well for me is either mint tea or rooibos tea. I use 4-5 teabags (mint or rooibos) per gallon. I'll put about ½ gallon of water in a pot on the stove, bring to a boil, drop in the tea bags and let it gently boil for about 5 minutes. I turn off the stove, let it sit for a couple of hours, come back and turn it on warm and add ¼ cup of sugar allowing the sugar to dissolve. Remove teabags and pour into a gallon jug filled with ice.

## Bottled Cinnamon Mint Tea (blazer 55)

Open a 2 oz. bottled water
Drop in 1 cinnamon stick
Add fresh mint (I used one 5" sprig)
Add a pinch of sugar *(optional)*

Reseal bottled water and shake vigorously. Set in sunny window for about an hour (like sun tea). When the hour is up, put in refrigerator to get good and cold. When ready to drink, strain and pour over ice.

# ICED COFFEE & COFFEE SUBSTITUTES

## Vanilla Iced Coffee (hnull2007)

low acid coffee (Puroast®, Simpatico)
vanilla syrup
cinnamon
nutmeg
milk
ice
whip cream

Cold brew your coffee the night before. In a glass, throw in a few ice cubes. Pour in a little coffee. Add sugar if you like, then dash of vanilla syrup, milk to taste. Mix thoroughly. Top off with your whip cream and a few dashes of cinnamon and nutmeg.

## Fake Mocha Latte (treekangaroo)

*So I finally made a hot drink that I think actually tastes good! It's like a mocha latte, but using carob chips and Cafix®.*

Sweetened carob chips
Cafix® coffee substitute
vanilla extract
milk
water

Put enough carob chips in the bottom of the mug to cover the bottom. Fill the mug halfway with milk and microwave until all of the carob chips melt. Fill the mug up the rest of the way with water and microwave until it is really hot (but be careful it doesn't overflow). Add a little less than a tsp of Cafix® and stir it in. Then add a few drops of vanilla extract, and it's done! I was disappointed in the hot carob drink by itself, but with the Cafix® and vanilla added it tastes really good!

# FRUIT SMOOTHIES

## Smoothies by Kadi

• I blended an Odwalla® carrot juice, some organic sliced pears *(packed in pear juice concentrate, but drained - you can save the juice &*

*use it for salad dressing by adding canola oil & a pinch of dried basil)* and ice cubes.

• I've made spinach or romaine with honeydew melon, which I wasn't immediately thrilled with, but found it much better when blended with ice. Since I teach elementary school & am surrounded by cold viruses, I'm glad to have a high nutrient drink.

• I've made a pear pumpkin smoothie (cottage cheese, canned pears in pear juice, organic canned pumpkin, nutmeg, vanilla, cinnamon & milk).

• I really liked the date smoothie (chopped fresh dates, cottage cheese, milk, vanilla), but it's very caloric so don't do that all the time.

## Strawberry Shortcake Smoothie (Carole)

4 oz. filtered water
1 cup sliced strawberries *(if can tolerate)*
1 cup vanilla frozen yogurt *(if can tolerate)*
2 tbsp. honey
1 graham cracker square
dash of cinnamon *(if can tolerate)*
1 cup ice

Blend in blender until smooth.

## Breakfast in a Glass (Carole)

*There are so many variations to this recipe if you can't tolerate the fruit listed, then use the one's you can tolerate. I also add 1 tbsp. of any powder greens you can tolerate. I use Kyo greens. You can also add sprouted flax or chia seeds. You can use yogurt instead of Kefir if you can tolerate it. The combinations are endless. Just make sure your choices are IC friendly.*

1 cup milk
½ cup blueberries
*1 banana (if can tolerate)*
½ cup raspberries *(if can tolerate)*
1 scoop protein powder *(I use Iso Natural by Allmax which is a 100% unflavored all natural whey protein)*
5 tbsp. Kefir *(if you can tolerate)*

Mix together in a blender and serve.

## Banana Natural Peanut Butter Smoothie (aprilchen)

*This makes a really, really healthy breakfast or meal substitution. It's super healthy because you're getting natural sugars and good carbohydrates from the banana and good protein from the natural peanut butter and whey or soy protein powder. This has also never made my IC flare and has actually calmed it when I felt like having a "cold" drink.*

1 serving of whey protein (vanilla flavored)
1 serving all natural (I use Earth Balance®) creamy peanut butter
½ cup soymilk or regular 1% milk
2 cups small or shaved ice
1 medium sized ripe organic or regular banana

Put all ingredients in a blender and blend on high about 1 minute until it forms a milkshake.

## Melon Juice (OllieR)

*This is a fruit juice that will allow you to vary your morning drink a little from pear and blueberry. Don't skip any ingredients. It needs them all!*

½ cup baby pear juice *(you can try regular pear juice but you may need to add some water then)*
1 cup watermelon
½ cup honeydew
2 tsp. sugar
Dash of sweet basil
Dash of coconut flakes

Put all ingredients in the blender and set to "liquefy." If it's too thick you can add some water (or alcohol if you can tolerate it!). You can strain it to get the coconut flakes out, but I found they were very small by the time they had been through the blender. Serve chilled. The recipe above made one large glass.

## Watermelon Icee (mystereys)

*This is a great summer drink & easy to make.*

Cut up watermelon, and freeze the chunks. When frozen, toss the watermelon cubes in a blender. Put in a little water, just enough so that it will blend. You can put a little sweetener in there if you want, but I find just the watermelon is sweet enough. Blend until you get a nice Icee or Slurpee consistency.

If you want to go fancy with it, you can pour it into a nice glass and top it off with a mint leaf for garnish. Now that I think about it, I wonder how a little mint blended in with the watermelon would taste.

## Pear Juice Freeze with Ginger and Vanilla (wagamama)

*This seemed more interesting than plain pear juice and it looks just like a frozen margarita. In fact, if you can tolerate a little vodka or rum, you might try blending it in. If you do this, tell me how it tastes!*

1 cup pear juice (I used R.W. Knudsen brand)
1 ½ cup ice
3 tbsp. ginger vanilla syrup *(recipe below)*

Combine all ingredients in blender and blend on high until smooth. You can serve it in a sugar-rimmed margarita glass if you're in that kind of mood. Makes 1 serving.

### Ginger Vanilla Syrup

*I used to make Pineapple Ginger Mojitos a lot before I had IC. I made a ginger flavored simple syrup for that too, so I adapted it to flavor this drink. I'm also thinking about adding some the next time I make peppermint iced tea.*

1 cup sugar
1 cup water
2 inches of fresh ginger, peeled*
1 vanilla bean

Chop ginger into large chunks. Combine all ingredients in a small saucepan and simmer over medium heat until sugar melts. Simmer on low for 10 minutes more, then remove from heat. Cool syrup to room temperature. Transfer to small covered container and refrigerate until cold or overnight. Strain solids from syrup using fine mesh strainer. Will keep in refrigerator up to one week. Makes 1 1/2 cups.

*\* Ginger is on the "try it" list. It's fine for me, but if you can't tolerate it, you can substitute another vanilla bean instead.*

# HERBAL & VEGGIE

## Sports Drink (sdm)

*Even when I was in remission I made my own sports drinks due to cost, control of ingredients, and convenience. But I always flavored it with a few sprinkles of unsweetened Kool Aid. With the first ingredient being citric acid, that is no longer an option. So, here is what I use now.*

½ cup blueberry juice
1 tbsp. sugar
¼ tsp. Morton® Lite Salt (sodium and potassium)
water to fill the rest of the bottle (mine is 16 oz.)

## Cucumber Basil Water (durangomandy)

I have been putting cucumber slices and crushed basil into a pitcher of cold water in the fridge. I tell myself it tastes like spa beverage. At least it's refreshing and a nice change from so much plain water. I don't tolerate mint well, but I think cucumber and mint would taste yummy, too.

## Infused Juice (Blazer)

*Recently I bought a Pampered Chef Tea Infuser. I thought I would try to make my own fruit juices using the IC diet list as a guide. I am sure you could adapt this recipe using fruits you can tolerate and by binding the fruit in cheesecloth or simple straining the juice.*

¼ cup blueberries
¼ cup mango
1 basil leaf
1 quart water
1 pack Stevia in the Raw (You can use regular sugar, honey or even Agave or drink plain whatever works for you.)

I followed the directions on the Infuser and left the fruit to infuse into the water overnight in the refrigerator. I separated the fruit and poured the juice into a glass with 1 pack of Stevia. Whoo Hoo! Fresh IC friendly juice and as the commercial says "It taste good, too."

*Editors note: Artificial sweeteners can be problematic for many patients. When in doubt, use some honey instead!*

## Peppermint water (cmcnatt)

My wife told me about a cold drink she heard about on the Dr. Oz show: peppermint water. Since I drink peppermint tea every day (my main hot drink since diagnosis of IC) I thought I'd try it for a change of pace summer cold drink. I grow peppermint so I take a couple of leaves and drop them in a container of water to put in the refrigerator. I like sweet things so I add Splenda and that's all. It is refreshing and something else I can add to my limited list of available drinks.

*Editors note: Artificial sweeteners can be problematic for many patients. When in doubt, use some honey instead!*

## Green Juice (kadi)

*This past week, I began starting my mornings with a cup of green juice. I don't have a juicer, so I've been shredding the romaine & chopping up the honeydew melon before putting it into my blender (or juicer) with a few ice cubes. I won't say this is my favorite beverage, but I will say that I feel really good for a few hours after drinking it AND everyone at work has been laid flat by a nasty cold, but I've just been sniffly for a few days.*

2 cups romaine lettuce, finely shredded
1 cup honeydew melon, chopped into dice cubes
3-5 ice cubes

Put into blender and puree until it makes juice! Since mornings are a little rushed sometimes, at night before going to bed, I shred the lettuce, chop the honeydew, put them into the blender and put that in the fridge until morning.

# ALCOHOLIC

## Coco Nut Martini (blazer 55)

1 can of root beer
vanilla vodka (a splash or a jigger, your choice)
3 oz. coconut milk
crushed ice
almonds that have been crushed into a powder

Put a little water in the bottom of a paper plate and then put the powdered almonds in the bottom of another paper plate. Dip the rim of a martini glass into the water and then into the powdered almonds leaving a dusting of the powder around the rim of the glass. Fill the martini glass with crushed ice. Pour in the coconut milk first and then add the vanilla vodka. Fill the glass up with root beer and stir vigorously.

## Hawaiian Hazelnut (hnull2007)

1 ½ cup vanilla ice cream
¼ cup chilled Puroast® low acid coffee
1 oz. Appleton White Rum
2 oz. Creme De Coconut liqueur
2 tbsp. Nutella®

Blend all ingredients well. Top off your drink with whip cream and a few dashes of cinnamon and nutmeg!!! yummy!

Feel free to make this non-alcoholic and so you don't miss out on the coconut flavor just add some coconut cream it does not have to be liqueur. You may adjust the amount of the ingredients this is just the way I like it. BOTTOMS UP.

cubes, blueberries, and almond slices. Spread the mixture evenly in the baking dish.

Blend the cottage cheese in a blender, food processor or using a hand mixer. When there is a smooth consistency, blend in the eggs and milk. Mix in the sugar and the extracts. Pour the liquid mixture over the top of the bread. For the best results, cover the casserole and let it sit for at least an hour (or up to overnight) in refrigerator.  Cover the French toast with aluminum foil and bake for 20 minutes. Remove the foil and bake for another 20 minutes until the casserole is puffy and golden brown. Serve and enjoy while still warm.

### Old Fashioned Pancake Recipe (Carole)

1 ½ cups all-purpose flour
3 ½ tsp. baking powder
1 tsp. salt
1 tbsp. white sugar
1 ¼ cups milk
1 egg
3 tbsp. butter, melted

In a large bowl, sift together the flour, baking powder, salt and sugar. Make a well in the center and pour in the milk, egg and melted butter; mix until smooth. Heat a lightly oiled griddle or frying pan over medium-high heat. Pour or scoop the batter onto the griddle, using approximately 1/4 cup for each pancake. Brown on both sides and serve hot.

### German Pancakes (Carole)

6 eggs
½ cup sugar
1 cup all purpose flour
½ tsp. vanilla
1 cup milk
½ cup butter
½ tsp. salt

Melt butter in a 11" x 13" (or 9" x 13") baking dish in the oven at 350 degrees. Blend eggs in a blender for at least 2 minutes. This is crucial to get the pancakes nice and thick. Add milk, flour, sugar, vanilla, and salt. Remove melted butter from oven and pour egg mixture over

# Breakfast & Brunch

## PANCAKES & FRENCH TOAST

### Baked Blueberry French Toast (Bladderella)

1 loaf hearty, whole wheat bread
1 cup blueberries
½ cup sliced almonds
½ cup Cottage Cheese
2 cups eggs or egg substitute
2 ½ cups skim milk
2 tbsp. granulated sugar
1 tsp. vanilla extract
¼ tsp. almond extract

Pre-heat the oven to 375 degrees. Lightly coat a 13" x 9" baking dish with non-stick spray.  Tear the bread into 1-inch cubes. Mix the bread melted butter. Bake at 400 degrees for 10-20 minutes. Batter and edges will rise up the edges of the pan. Serve with pure maple syrup.

## Cinnamon Peach Pancakes (Carole)

2 cups flour
1 tbsp. sugar
1 tsp. salt
1 tsp. baking soda
1 tsp. cinnamon *(if can tolerate)*
¾ tsp. baking powder
2 eggs
2 cups buttermilk *(if can tolerate)*
1 tbsp. melted butter plus additional butter for the grill or skillet
2 peaches - peeled, pitted and diced *(if can tolerate)*

In a medium bowl, whisk together flour, sugar, salt, baking soda, cinnamon, and baking powder. In a large bowl, beat eggs. Add buttermilk and melted butter. Mix to combine.

## Ricotta-Cottage Cheese Pancakes (Diane M)

1 cup all-purpose flour
1 tbsp. granulated sugar
¼ tsp. salt
1 tsp. baking powder
4 eggs
1 cup ricotta cheese
1 cup small-curd cottage cheese
¾ cup non-fat milk
1 tsp. vanilla extract
1 tsp. grated lemon rind *(if can tolerate)*

Combine the flour, sugar, salt, and baking powder in a large bowl. In a separate bowl beat the eggs with the ricotta, cottage cheese, milk, vanilla, and lemon zest. Add this mixture to the flour mixture, stirring until moistened. Do not stir any more than necessary to thoroughly combine ingredients. Drop a small amount on a lightly greased griddle or skillet over moderate heat and turn when the edges appear golden brown and dry, and the surface is bubbly. Makes about 24 3" to 4" inch pancakes.

## Stuffed French Toast (Diane M)

12 slices of bread
12 eggs
2 cups of milk
16 oz. of cream cheese, softened
1 tsp. of vanilla

Cube bread and set aside. Mix eggs, milk, cream cheese and vanilla together in a bowl. Grease a 9x13 inch pan and then line it with the following: Add 1 layer of bread cubes, spread evenly; 1/2 of the liquid mixture, and pour evenly. Add the rest of the bread cubes, spread evenly; add the rest of the liquid mixture, spread evenly. Refrigerate overnight. The next morning, take it out and let it warm to room temperature (very important). Then bake in a 375 oven for 45 min.

## Rockin French Toast (Ollie R)

Hawaiian sweet bread, cut into nice thick slices
1 egg
splash of milk
¾ tbsp. cinnamon
½ -1 tbsp. white sugar

Whisk the liquid ingredients. Dip in the bread and heat on a pan or griddle. I do not use Pam® or butter and it does not stick. I lightly spread on butter after and top lightly with powdered sugar. It does not bother my IC but I'm not sure if the bread would bother anybody who is extremely diet sensitive. Make sure to check the label.

## Gluten, Egg, and Dairy Free Blueberry Pancakes (Sarah1982)

½ cup rice flour
½ cup buckwheat flour
½ cup corn flour
¼ cup ground flax seeds *(optional)*
2 tsp. baking powder
1 tsp. baking soda
¼ tsp. salt
rice milk *(I just kept adding the rice milk until I reach a consistency that I liked)*
½ cup blueberries *(I probably used MUCH more. I just keep adding until it seemed like a good amount)*

1 tsp. pure vanilla extract

I keep things quick and simple, so mixed together all dry ingredients. Add vanilla. Gradually add rice milk until batter is not too thick, but not runny. Fold in desired amount of blueberries. I just use cooking spray and cooked in a skillet till nice and golden brown. Enjoy with some maple syrup!

## Simple Pear Brunch (Blazer)

Pear
Sliced Almonds
Italian Bread
Ricotta Cheese
Sea salt and black pepper (*optional*)

Toast a ½ inch slice of Italian Bread. Spread generous amount of Ricotta cheese on toast. Place slices of pear onto ricotta cheese toast. Sprinkle with sliced almonds.

# QUICHE & EGG DISHES

## Vegetarian Quiche (Squirrel)

Preheat oven to 180 degrees Celsius or about 370 degrees Fahrenheit. I use a pre-made rolled quiche crust or homemade quiche/pie crust (about 12-13 oz. or 400 g). Unroll and lay on a baking paper sheet. Then create an edge or corner. Cut 3-4 small or 1-2 large spring onions into thin strips and fry them in 1 tbsp. of walnut oil for about 1 or 2 minutes until they are soft but not quite brown and evenly divide the onions on the quiche crust.

Mix 400 g or 12 to 13 oz. of plain cream cheese with 1 egg and 1 egg yolk, IC-friendly herbs that you like and season with salt and half a tsp. of sugar and beat mixture with an egg beater. Pour mixture over onions and top with about 100 g or 3-4 oz. of grated Mozzarella cheese. Bake until light golden brown, let cool for 10 minutes and serve with a salad.

## Asparagus Quiche (Carole)

½ to ¾ lb. asparagus, trimmed, chopped
water
2 tbsp. butter
½ cup chopped mushrooms

4 green onions, with green, thinly sliced (*if can tolerate*)
1 ½ cups shredded mild Cheddar cheese
4 large eggs
1 ½ cups half-and-half or whole milk
½ tsp. salt
1/8 tsp. ground black pepper (*if can tolerate*)
dash nutmeg (*if can tolerate*)
1 (9 inch) unbaked pie crust (*I make my own*)

In a saucepan, cover asparagus with water. Bring to a boil over high heat; reduce heat, cover, and cook for 5 minutes. Drain and set aside. In a skillet, heat butter over medium-low heat; add mushrooms. Sauté until mushrooms are tender; add green onions and cook for 1 minute longer. Set aside.

Baked pie crust at 375° for 8 minutes. Remove from oven and reduce oven temperature to 350°. Arrange vegetables and shredded cheese in pie pastry. Whisk together the eggs and half-and-half; add salt, pepper, and nutmeg. Pour egg mixture over the vegetables. Place the filled pie shell on a large cookie sheet or jelly-roll pan. Place in the oven and cook for 45 to 55 minutes, or until a knife inserted in the center comes out clean.

## Broccoli Quiche (Carole)

2 tbsp. butter
1 onion or chives, minced (*if can tolerate*)
1 tsp. minced garlic
2 cups chopped fresh broccoli
1 (9 inch) unbaked pie crust (*I make my own*)
1 ½ cups shredded Mozzarella cheese
4 eggs, well beaten
1 ½ cups milk
1 tsp. salt
½ tsp. black pepper (*if can tolerate*)
1 tbsp. butter, melted

Preheat oven to 350 degrees F (175 degrees C). Over medium-low heat melt butter in a large saucepan. Add onions, garlic and broccoli. Cook slowly, stirring occasionally until the vegetables are soft. Spoon vegetables into crust and sprinkle with cheese. Combine eggs and milk. Season with salt and pepper. Stir in melted butter. Pour egg mixture over vegetables and cheese. Bake in preheated oven for 30 minutes, or until center has set.

### Egg Scrambles (Kadi)

*I like omelettes but I'm neither coordinated nor patient, so I just make these as scrambles. I've really liked these combinations. Enjoy!*

**Zucchini Basil:** Sauté thin slices of zucchini (½ cup) in olive oil with a sprinkle of garlic & dried basil. When the zucchini is almost cooked, add one whole egg & one egg white (beaten) and an oz. of low fat shredded Mozzarella. Cook to desired texture.

**Turkey/Broccoli/Cheese:** Heat 1 tsp. of Land O'Lakes butter with canola in a small frying pan. Add ½ cup fresh or frozen broccoli florets & cook until soft. Take out 1-2 slices of Hormel Naturals® Oven Roasted Turkey, cut it into 1" square pieces, & add them to the skillet to heat them up. Then add the beaten egg (1 whole egg, 1-2 egg whites), and 1 oz. shredded Mozzarella. Cook until eggs are done.

**Asparagus, Mushroom & Cream Cheese:** Cut asparagus into 2" long pieces, cut a mushroom into thin slices. Sauté asparagus in butter or oil until tender crisp, sauté mushrooms until lightly golden. Then add the beaten egg and a tbsp. of Philly light ⅓ less fat cream cheese' & cook until eggs are done to your preference. Be sure to use the cream cheese in the block form not the tub, which has acidic preservatives.

**Red Bell Pepper, Pinto Beans, Corn Tortilla, Mozzarella:** Cook diced red bell peppers (¼ cup) in canola oil until soft, add 1/2 cup pinto beans (Safeway Organics is a good brand with no preservatives) & heat through. Add thin strips of corn tortilla (be sure to buy an acid-free tortilla--Trader Joe's truly handmade corn tortillas), & cook until golden brown. Add beaten egg (1 whole egg, 1 egg white) & ¼ cup Mozzarella. Cook evenly. Serve with a spoonful of Philly Light Cream Cheese (block form, not tub).

### Mini Frittatas (stacey79)

3 large eggs
2 tbsp. milk
2 tbsp. grated Parmesan cheese
¼ cup diced onion
¾ cup diced broccoli (*if using frozen broccoli, thaw first in microwave then dice*)

Preheat oven to 375 degrees. Spray or grease muffin tins. Whisk the eggs and milk together. Add the cheese, onion and broccoli. Pour egg mixture into muffin tins until ⅔ full. Bake for 12 to 14 minutes or until edges are slightly golden. Cool and serve. Makes 8 frittatas. You can use the same mixture to make 12 with a mini muffin pan if desired.

everything is well combined, then season with salt and white pepper to taste. Moisten your hands a bit, then divide the mixture into four patties. Make each patty as big as your palm, then press to flatten. Store the patties in your fridge for at least 20 minutes; doing so will help the patties firm up and stay together when you fry them.

Heat one to two tsp. of coconut oil in a pan over medium heat. Fry the burgers for 4-5 minutes on each side. Make sure the burgers are cooked through. They are ready to eat when they are golden brown and a little crispy on both sides. The burgers reheat well and are also good cold.

### Steak Sandwich (Kadi)

Pan cook thinly sliced steak and red bell pepper in a frying pan with a sprinkle of garlic powder, salt, oregano & a tiny amount of black pepper (if tolerated). Separately sauté thin sliced mushrooms in canola oil. Put the steak, red bell pepper, mushrooms on a 3/4" thick slice of artisan bread, then put a slice of Mozzarella cheese on top & microwaved it for 30 seconds to melt it. Topped it with another slice of bread and it made a delicious steak sandwich. Took about 10 minutes total, including slicing the meat & vegetables, cooking the ingredients and melting the cheese. Looking forward to making this again.

### Grilled Peanut Butter Apple Sandwich (Carole)

1 IC friendly apple, peeled, cored, and thinly sliced
½ tsp. white sugar
½ tsp. ground cinnamon *(if can tolerate)*
8 tbsp. creamy peanut butter
8 slices IC friendly bread
¼ cup butter

Mix cinnamon and sugar together in a small bowl. Spread one tablespoon of peanut butter onto one side of 8 slices of bread. Arrange apple slices on 4 slices of bread. Sprinkle the cinnamon/sugar mixture evenly over the

# Burgers, Sandwiches & Pizza

### Chicken Burgers (mareng9)

1 lb. chicken minced
½ cup finely chopped coriander.
½ cup finely chopped mint or 1 tsp. dried mint
1 tsp. ground cumin
1 tsp. garlic powder
2 tbsp. gluten-free breadcrumbs
1 egg *(to bind)*
sea salt and white pepper
coconut oil *(for frying)*

Combine the mince or shredded, cooked chicken with the herbs, spices and breadcrumbs. Beat the egg and add it. Mix until

apples. Top with the remaining 4 slices of bread, peanut butter face down.
Melt the butter in a large skillet over medium heat. Fry sandwiches until browned, about 1 to 2 minutes on each side.

## Grilled Bacon Apple Sandwich (Carole)

6 slices nitrate free bacon
5 tablespoons peanut butter
4 slices IC friendly bread
5 tbsp. IC friendly apricot jam (if can tolerate. Can substitute with other IC friendly jams)
pepper to taste and tolerance
1 IC friendly apple, cored and thinly sliced
3 tbsp. softened butter

Place the bacon in a large, deep skillet, and cook over medium-high heat, turning occasionally, until evenly browned, about 10 minutes. Drain the bacon slices on a paper towel-lined plate. Spread the peanut butter onto two slices of bread. Spread the jam onto the remaining two slices of bread, and sprinkle with pepper to taste. Arrange half of the cooked bacon and half of the sliced apple onto each jam-covered bread sliced. Top with the peanut butter smeared pieces of bread. Heat a large skillet over medium heat. Spread the butter over the outside of the sandwiches and place into the preheated skillet. Cook until golden brown on both sides. Enjoy!

## Ham and Pear Sandwich (Carole)

4 slices IC friendly bread
1 tbsp. IC friendly pear jam (optional)
6 slices nitrate free ham
1 pear, peeled and thinly sliced
2 dashes ground black pepper to taste and tolerance
1 cup shredded mozzarella cheese
1 tbsp. butter

Spread pear jam on bread slices. Layer each with 3 slices of ham, half of the pear slices, a dash of pepper, and ½ cup mozzarella cheese. Top with remaining bread. Lightly spread butter on the outer sides of each sandwich. Heat a skillet or griddle over medium heat. Grill the sandwiches until the cheese is melted

and the bread is golden brown, about 3 minutes per side. Cut each sandwich in half to serve.

## Beets, Spinach, and Goat Cheese Sandwich (Carole)

4 small beets
2 tbsp. olive oil
2 bunches spinach, trimmed (about 12 cups)
salt and black pepper to taste
1 tbsp. Mock red wine vinegar dressing (see below)
4 oz. goat cheese
¼ cup chopped raisins (as tolerated)
4 rolls, split

Heat oven to 450° F. Wrap the beets in a large piece of aluminum foil and bake until easily pierced with a paring knife, 35 to 45 minutes. Let cool, then, using a paper towel, remove the skins. Thinly slice. Heat the oil in a large skillet over medium-high heat. Add as much spinach as will fit in the skillet. Season with salt and pepper. Cook, tossing frequently and adding more spinach when there is room, until just wilted, 2 to 3 minutes. Stir in the dressing. Meanwhile, combine the goat cheese, raisins, and pepper in a small bowl. Divide the sliced beets, spinach, and goat cheese spread among the rolls.

Mock Red Wine Salad Dressing
2 tbsp. olive oil
1 tbsp. blueberry juice
½ tsp. white sugar

Mix well and Serve

## ● Bean Cakes in Lettuce Wraps or Corn Tortillas (Briza)

Super easy recipe! Very healthy and filling. Dairy free, gluten free, no added oil, lotsa fiber, all whole foods, and vegan.

1 can beans drained and rinsed (I use pinto, black, or kidney beans)
¼ cup water
1 cup dry oatmeal (not instant)
½ cup or more shredded raw carrots or sweet potato

22

½ cup roasted and peeled red bell pepper (*optional*)
¼ cup minced parsley or cilantro (*optional*)
Salt, or pepper, coconut aminos, or any herbs and seasonings that you like

Rinse and drain beans then put in glass bowl with ¼ cup water. Microwave until very hot. Mash the beans with a potato or bean masher, or a large fork or large spoon. Mix in everything else.
Season with salt, pepper and other herbs to taste. Put in fridge for 1 hour or overnight to set.

Preheat oven to 425 F. Line a cookie sheet or other oven safe pan with parchment paper. Make bean cake patties whatever size you like ( I make mine about 3" diameter) and arrange with space between each on parchment paper. Place in oven and Cook for about 15-20 minutes then turn them over and cook another 15 minutes or so until both sides are browned and toasty outside, but still soft inside. You can also cook them in a preheated non-stick or iron skillet with no oil needed. I've found the oven baked on parchment paper turn out better.

Eat them hot or let cool. They're great at room temp and even cold. They travel well when packed for a lunch to go, even without an ice pack they are fine for several hours.  I serve them in romaine leaves or corn tortillas. Topped with avocado, shredded cabbage, and whatever kind of topping you want. Roasted red bell pepper sauce in lieu of hot sauce works great. .

Dairy free roasted red bell pepper sauce
2 red bell peppers, roasted, skinned, and deseeded
2 cloves roasted garlic (optional)
¼ cup raw unsalted cashews or raw unsalted sunflower seeds, soaked in water for 30 mins to soften

Drain cashews or sunflower seeds. Put everything in blender and purée til smooth. You may need to add a small splash of water, maybe not. (If you add too much water you can

always thicken it by cooking it down In a saucepan). Salt to taste if you use salt.

## Greek Gyros (Raiinbow Eyes)

**Gyro Meat:**
1 medium onion
1 pound ground lamb
1 pound ground beef
1 tbsp. garlic
1 tbsp. dried marjoram
1 tbsp. dried ground rosemary
1 tsp. salt
1 tsp. freshly ground black pepper (*if tolerated*)
1 tsp. dried oregano
1 tsp. ground cumin (*if tolerated*)
1 tsp. ground dried thyme

**Tzatziki Sauce:**
16 oz. plain yogurt, greek
1 medium cucumber, peeled, seeded, and finely chopped
Pinch of salt
4 cloves garlic, minced
1 tbsp. olive oil
5 to 6 mint leaves, finely minced

**Fixings:**
Pita bread
cucumber slices (*optional*)
lettuce or leafy green of your choosing (*optional*)
feta cheese (*optional*)

Gyro Meat instructions:
Place the onion in a food processor, and process until finely chopped. Scoop the onions onto the center of a towel, gather up the ends of the towel, and squeeze out the liquid from the onions. Place the onions into a mixing bowl along with the lamb and beef. Season with the garlic, oregano, cumin,  marjoram, rosemary, thyme, black pepper, and salt. Mix well with your hands until well combined. Cover and refrigerate 1 to 2 hours to allow the flavors to blend. Let sit covered overnight if you wish.

Preheat oven to 325 degrees F (165 degrees C). Place the meat mixture into the food processor, and pulse for about a minute until finely chopped and the mixture feels tacky. Pack the meat mixture into a 7x4 inch loaf pan, making sure there are no air pockets. Line a roasting pan with a damp kitchen towel. Place the loaf pan on the towel, inside the roasting pan, and place into the preheated oven. Fill the roasting pan with boiling water to reach halfway up the sides of the loaf pan.

Bake until the gyro meat is no longer pink in the center, and the internal temperature registers 165 degrees F (75 degrees C) on a meat thermometer, 45 minutes to 1 hour. Pour off any accumulated fat, and allow to cool slightly. Drain any additional fat from the pan. Remove the loaf from the pan and cut into thin slices.

Tzatziki Sauce instructions:
Place the yogurt in a tea towel or cheese cloth, gather up the edges, suspend over a bowl, and drain for 2 hours in the refrigerator. Place the chopped cucumber in a tea towel (strong paper towels also work) and squeeze to remove the liquid; discard liquid. In a medium mixing bowl, combine the drained yogurt, cucumber, salt, garlic, olive oil, and mint.

Assemble the gyro with the pita bread and tzatziki sauce. I spread the sauce all over the inside of the pita (you may want to use less), slices of meat, and desired toppings. Fold over to eat, and enjoy!

*Tip: To reheat gyro meat, instead of microwaving it, use skillet with a light drizzle of olive oil to brown each side while reheating. It tastes much better reheated that way*

## Japanese Onigiri - Rice Balls (Nihon)

*I live in Japan and often eat onigiri for lunch. It is great for picnics or packed lunches. Here is a basic recipe.*

steamed Japanese rice
strips of dried nori (seaweed)
salt to taste
canned tuna fish or grilled salmon (small chunks)

Cook steamed rice. Put about a half cup of steamed rice in a bowl. Make a dent in the center of the rice and place fillings. Wet your hands in water so that the rice won't stick. Rub

some salt on your hands. Place the rice in the rice bowl on your hands. Form the rice into a round or a triangle, by pressing lightly with your both palms. Wrap the rice ball with a strip of nori. I also like to mix sesame seeds in with the rice or sprinkle some on the outside.

## Mini Pizza's (SweetPea85)

*I just made a fantastic pizza last night and you can either make it mini on Natures Own® English muffins or you can make it whole using regular dough. Last night I made them mini and it was so DELISH!*

English muffins
Alfredo sauce
spinach leaves
ricotta cheese
cooked chicken pieces

Cut each English muffin into half's and you should end up with 12 total. Put some Alfredo sauce on each one I put like a big spoon full *(don't over do it though)* then I add a spinach leaf on each, then one spoon full of ricotta cheese on each and then cooked chicken pieces on each and then layer each mini pizza with Mozzarella cheese and put into the oven 350 degrees for 15-20 minutes or until the English muffins get a little crispy and it looks done on top. ENJOY! Best mini pizzas ever!

## Easy Whole Wheat Pizza Dough (Bladderella)

1 ¼ cup white flour
2 ¼ tsp. yeast
½ tsp. salt
2 tbsp. oil
1 cup warm water (not boiling)
1 cup whole wheat flour

Preheat the oven to 375 degrees. Combine the white flour, yeast, and salt in a large mixing bowl. Add the oil and warm water to the mixture and combine with an electric mixer. Mix on high speed for several minutes until a soft, elastic dough forms. Stir in the whole wheat flour gradually, by hand. When it's all incorporated, you should be able to easily pick up the dough and knead it gently until you get a soft dough ball. I did this right in the bowl – that's the benefit of a large mixing bowl! Set aside in a warm place and cover with plastic wrap or even just a dish towel. Let the dough rise for about 10-15 minutes.

Roll out the dough into two 12-inch circles. Poke with forks to prevent bubbling. Place on a baking sheet or if you're really fancy and cool, a pizza stone. You can add toppings and then bake for about 12-15 minutes, or you can just bake the crust ahead of time and add your toppings later. If you're baking the crust with the toppings on it, turn the broiler on for the last few minutes of baking to get a lightly crispy outside crust.

## Nomato Pizza Sauce (Carole)

1 14 oz. can of sweet potato puree (or you can do 1½ - 2 cups fresh cooked)
1 14 oz. can of beets drained
1 14 oz. can of pears drained
1 cup pure pear juice (make sure IC friendly)
3 roasted red peppers

To roast red peppers
Coat them with olive oil then add oregano, garlic powder, basil, pepper, sea salt and whatever kind of seasoning you want and can tolerate. Use lots. Cook until tender. I then put them in a container for 15 minutes to loosen skin then I peel them.

Put all Nomato ingredients into a blender and puree. I then add more seasonings to taste. Simmer on stove top for a while to increase the flavors. Spread on crust then add more oregano. It makes a great tasting pizza sauce. I have also posted a Pizza recipe with a creamy garlic sauce that is also really good. Good luck I hope you like it.

## Spinach Sesame Pizza (sasapippi)

pizza dough (Trader Joe's with no preservatives but any basic pizza dough will do)
10 oz. frozen chopped spinach
2 tbsp. olive oil
1 bunch green onions finely chopped (leave these out if you can't tolerate them)
2 garlic cloves finely chopped

4-5 oz. feta cheese, crumbled
salt to taste (and pepper if you can handle it)
Mozzarella cheese
sesame seeds

Preheat oven to 425. Thaw the spinach and squeeze well to remove excess water. In medium saucepan, heat oil. Add onions and garlic. Cook, stirring about two minutes. Add spinach and half the feta. Stir well and salt to taste. Spread the mixture on the dough, add the rest of the feta, as many sesame seeds as you like and the Mozzarella. Bake for 20 minutes until golden brown.

## Crustless Veggie Pizza (Diane M)

Make a layer of home made mashed potatoes, topped with a layer of raw shredded vegetables (sweet potato, yellow squash and carrots tonight) tossed in a couple of spoons of olive oil. Put under the broiler for about 7 or minutes, not so close that they'll burn, then take it out, top with fresh Mozzarella cheese and stick under the broiler until it melts. MMMMM! Sort of like a veggie pizza with a mashed potato crust.

## Pizza with a Creamy Garlic Sauce  (Carole)

2 cups all purpose white flour
1 cup warm water
⅓ cup granulated white sugar (I used ¼ C)
1 package active dry yeast
1 tsp. salt

Add all dry ingredients together in a large bowl. Stir in one cup warmed water. Use a wooden spoon to mix well and form a dough. Cover bowl with a towel or plastic wrap and set aside someplace warm. Give the dough about 30 minutes to rise and it should roughly double in size from the action of the yeast. Lightly coat countertop with flour for rolling the dough out. Transfer dough to the clean area and knead gently about 10 times. Then begin to shape the dough into a circular shape. Use a rolling pin to further flatten and shape the dough until it is about 1/2 inch thick. Roll it out thinner, about ⅓ inch thick, if you want a thinner, crispier crust. Transfer prepared crust to a pizza pan.

Creamy Garlic Pizza Sauce
1 cup heavy cream
1-2 tsp. garlic
2 tbsp. butter
1 tbsp. (approx) flour or cornstarch to thicken
Heat in pot until thickened then spread on pizza crust

Assembly Instructions
I sprinkled oregano and basil all over the crust on top of sauce. I then add Mozzarella cheese. You can then top with whatever toppings you like. I put mushrooms, red peppers, onion (I pre-fried these in a pan with butter) and I had some roasted red peppers in the freezer I also put on. I wanted to add black olives but I didn't have any. Baked in oven at 450 until crust was golden brown and cheese was melted.

*I also melted 3tbsp. of butter and added garlic powder so I could dip my stuffed crust ends into it.*

## Creamy Feta Pizza Sauce (missisola)

*Today I was planning to have chicken but I had an accident in the kitchen and let's just say I had to plan a new dinner. I decided to make pizza since I had mushrooms from yesterday in my fridge as well as cheese and I also bought these new Tortilla pizza breads that I wanted to try. I searched here for a recipe and found one but it contained stuff I could not tolerate xso I made another version*

feta cheese
cream
a little butter
dried oregano

Mix together and use as sauce for pizza.

## Watermelon-Pepper Pizza Sauce (mrmambo)

*Still working on developing a nomato sauce recipe that can fool me and my wife. I've tried many of the ones online and find the beets give it a cloying sweetness that I don't love. I reached out to Harold McGee, a renowned food scientist and author, who suggested trying **watermelon**. He said "You might try cooking down fresh red watermelon, which has the same red pigment and develops a similar aroma on cooking (though*

*admittedly with a squash-like overtone from being in that family), maybe in combination with red bell peppers (different pigment but same family as tomato).*

Watermelon:
2 lbs. watermelon chunks, pureed in processor (4 lbs w/ rind)
- simmered until thickened, about 90 minutes
- reduced down to 6 oz. (wt.)

Peppers:
3 mixed bell peppers (red, yellow, orange)
- tossed with oil and roasted at 350° until soft, about 45 min
- placed in bowl with plastic wrap for 15 min to remove skins
- pureed, resulting in about 6 oz. (wt.)

Mixed both purees, then added pizza spices.

For Marinara Pizza Sauce:
1.5 tsp. dried parsley
1 tsp. dried basil
½ tsp. dried oregano
¼ tsp. dried thyme
1/8 tsp. black pepper
2 tbsp. olive oil
1 tbsp. garlic powder
1 ¼ tsp. salt

Other ingredients:
8 oz. mushrooms
3-6 green onions
Chopped and sautéd in pan until brown, about 7-9 min.

# Sauces, Marinades, Relish & Jelly

## SAUCES & GRAVY

### Alfredo Sauce (Carole)

*There is nothing better than an Alfredo sauce made without flour that thickens just with all that wonderful cheese. Super tasty!*

1 cup butter
2 cups heavy cream
salt and pepper to taste *(if can tolerate)*
1 dash garlic powder
¾ cup grated Romano cheese *(if can tolerate)*
½ cup grated Parmesan cheese *(if can tolerate)*

In a large saucepan, melt butter into cream over low heat. Add salt, pepper and garlic. Stir

in cheese over medium heat until melted. The sauce will thicken. Serve immediately over cooked pasta.

### Homemade Enchilada & Taco Sauce (Bladderella)

2 tbsp. vegetable or canola oil
2 tbsp. all-purpose or gluten-free flour
4 tbsp. chili powder *(use less if you think this is too much for you)*
½ tsp. garlic powder
½ tsp. salt
½ tsp. cumin
¼ tsp. oregano
2 cups chicken or vegetable stock

Heat oil in a small saucepan over medium-high heat. Add flour and stir together over the heat for one minute. Stir in the remaining seasonings. Gradually add in the stock, whisking constantly to remove lumps. Reduce heat and simmer 10-15 minutes until thick. Use immediately or refrigerate in an airtight container for up to two weeks.

### Red Bell Pepper Sauce (Phoenix Girl)

*Use as an IC-friendly replacement for tomato-based sauces on pizza, pasta, etc.*

2-3 red bell peppers
1 carrot, peeled
¼ onion*
3 cloves garlic
2 cups low-sodium chicken broth
salt
Italian herb seasoning
Parmesan cheese, grated

Roast the vegetables on the grill or under the broiler. Coat everything in olive oil and grill/broil close to the heat, turning occasionally. The carrot, onion, and garlic should be tender, and the skin of the peppers will need to be blistered and charred. Once the peppers are done, put them in a paper bag, fold the top to seal in the steam, and let sit. After 15 minutes, peel the skin off of the peppers, remove the stem and the seeds, and toss the meat of the peppers, along with any pepper juice from the cutting board, into a blender with the rest of the veggies and puree. Combine the vegetable puree with the chicken broth in a medium saucepan and bring to a simmer. Add salt, Parmesan, and herbs to taste. Simmer about 30 minutes, or until sauce thickens. Makes about 1 quart.

*If you're sensitive to onion, leave it out and sub in 3-5 more cloves of garlic.*

## Roasted Orange Bell Pepper and Garlic Sauce (Briza)

*I made a mesquite fire in the pit tonight to grill some veggies and threw this sauce together. I do NOT like bell peppers, but bought these orange ones only because they were so pretty! This sauce turned out AWESOME and so creamy, sweet, and had only they slightest bell peppery-taste! I intended to use it as a veggie dip or on pasta but it was so good I ate it all straight from the bowl!!!*

4 orange bell peppers
1 head garlic
¼ cup almonds (optional)
1 tbsp. olive oil or water

Wrap entire head of garlic in foil and put on grate or place in coals and cook until very soft. These will cook faster in the coals so be careful not to burn. Place peppers on grate and roast over flame, turning often until all sides are blackened. Place in plastic bag for 10 minutes to steam and loosen skin. Remove from bag and peel off blackened skin with your fingers or by scraping with a knife. Remove seeds. Remove garlic from foil, slice top off with knife, and squeeze the head to remove the softened pulp. Puree pulp, peppers, almonds, and oil/water til very smooth.

## Creamy Cauliflower Sauce (Bladderella)

8 large cloves garlic, minced
2 tbsp. butter
5-6 cups cauliflower florets
6-7 cups vegetable broth or water
1 tsp. salt *(more to taste)*
½ tsp. pepper *(more to taste)*
½ cup milk *(more to taste)*

**Garlic:** Sauté the minced garlic with the butter in a large nonstick skillet over low heat. Cook for several minutes or until the garlic is soft and fragrant but not browned. Browned or burnt garlic will taste bitter. Remove from heat and set aside.

**Cauliflower:** Bring the water or vegetable broth to a boil in a large pot. Add the cauliflower and cook, covered, for 7-10 minutes or until cauliflower is fork tender. Do not drain.

**Puree:** Use a slotted spoon to transfer the cauliflower pieces to the blender. Add 1 cup vegetable broth or cooking liquid, sautéed garlic/butter, salt, pepper, and milk. Blend or puree for several minutes until the sauce is very smooth, adding more broth or milk depending on how thick you want the sauce. You may have to do this in batches depending on the size of your blender. Serve hot! *(If the sauce starts to look dry, add a few drops of water, milk, or olive oil).*

*Notes*
*• Adding a little bit of olive oil will enhance the flavor and help keep the sauce really smooth. You can also add Parmesan cheese.*
*• The sauce will "dry out" a little bit as it cools on the pasta. Adding a little water to the leftovers will help make it creamy again.*
*• Combine cauliflower sauce with cooked fettuccini noodles in a large pot or skillet for a delicious main course.*
*• Mix with brown rice and top with Mozzarella cheese for a yummy side dish.*

## Raisin Sauce To Serve With Ham (Carole)

1 ½ cups water
¾ cup organic untreated brown raisins(if can tolerate)
⅓ cup packed brown sugar
1 tsp. cornstarch
1 pinch salt

Bring water to a boil in a saucepan. Stir raisins into water, reduce heat to medium, and boil until very tender, about 5 minutes. Whisk brown sugar, cornstarch, and salt into raisin mixture and simmer until thickened, about 10 minutes.

## Mushroom Gravy (agilityme)

8 oz. Baby Bella Mushrooms, sliced
2 cup roasted vegetable stock (*See recipe in soup section*)
2 tbsp. butter or olive oil
2 tbsp. cornstarch
salt to taste
pepper to taste (*if tolerated*)

Coat large pan with either olive oil or butter. Add a single layer of sliced mushrooms. Brown one side, flip and brown the other side. Be sure not to crowd the pan or your mushrooms will not brown. It is better to do two batches than to crowd the pan. Add more butter or oil as needed. Set browned mushrooms aside. Pour cold roasted vegetable stock into a medium sized pan. Whisk in the cornstarch. Bring to a boil stiffing constantly. Reduce heat, continue to stir, add mushrooms and simmer until gravy thickens.

## Nomato Sauce (loveslife)

1 15 oz. can of whole beets drained
1 30 oz. can of yams drained and rinsed well (*or equivalent in cooked carrots*)
1 15 oz. can of pears in pear juice
3 roasted red bell peppers (*This may not be IC friendly for some. Obviously don't add them if you can't tolerate them! You could try subbing pureed carrots for them if need be.*)
1 tsp. lemon oil (*may be IC tolerated may not, again use caution*)
1 tsp. salt

I first puree each of the above in my Cuisinart®, making sure you use the pear juice that comes in the can also. Mix all into a pot with the lemon oil and salt. Simmer on low for about 30 minutes. Then I do a final puree in my blender. I freeze in baggies what I'm not going to use right away. It doesn't look like much but when cooked into other things it's quite wonderful.

## Nomato Ketchup (loveslife)

2 cups nomato sauce
½ cup corn syrup
½ cup raw sugar
1 tsp. salt

2 heaping tsp. allspice
1 garlic clove crushed
3 tbsp. onion finally chopped
2 tsp. lemon oil flavoring
vegetable oil

Sauté onion and garlic in a little vegetable oil until translucent. Add remaining ingredients. Cook on low heat for about 1/2 an hour, stirring occasionally so doesn't stick, until mixture thickens and darkens. Puree in blender, pour into containers and keep in fridge.

# MARINADES, RELISH & JELLY

## Root Beer Meat Marinade (Carole)

*Because we cannot tolerate store bought meat marinades I came up with this recipe. I like it best on steak but you can use it on any meat you want.*

I can or small bottle caffeine free Root Beer
½ tsp. garlic
¼ cup vegetable oil
½ tsp. basil
3-6 large garlic cloves crushed
1 large onion chopped (*if can tolerate*)
½ tsp. pepper
1 tsp. salt or sea salt
1 tsp. unsulfured molasses

Mix together and pour over meat and marinade for several hours or overnight in a sealed container. Hope you enjoy it.

## Non-Cranberry Thanksgiving Relish (sunflower23)

¾ cup pomegranate juice or a berry juice of your choice
12 oz. any frozen berries/fruit (raspberries work well because they're tart)
3 oz. box of raspberry jello

Pour juice into a sauce pan and heat until it just starts to boil. Add frozen berries. Keep at a low boil for 10 minutes, stirring occasionally. Add raspberry jello and stir until dissolved. Refrigerate 4 hours or overnight.

## Cabbage Condiment (Carole)

*I don't know about you but I miss vinegar terribly. I am also always at a loss as to what to put on a sandwich. I think I came up with something pretty tasty last night that was reminiscent of a vinegary condiment. I used some juice from Bubbie's Kosher dill pickles. These are pickles that don't have any vinegar in them. I am not too fond of the pickles themselves but have been trying to come up with something to use the sour juice in.*

2 cups of red cabbage sliced thinly
enough apple cider to just cover the cabbage
and about ¼ cup of water (the apple cider I use is just apples, nothing else added)
1/8 cup of Bubbie's pickle juice
about 5 allspice berries
a little salt and pepper if you can handle it

Bring to a boil and then turn down and simmer until most of the liquid is gone and the cabbage is soft. Don't forget to remove the allspice berries before eating. I made some homemade veggie burgers and put this cabbage on top. It was really good.

## Easy Blueberry Jelly (HRJ)

6 cups fresh berries
1 cup water
½ cup coconut sugar *(maybe less if you use regular).*

I put 3 cups of berries, ½ cup of water and the sugar in a sauce pan and brought to a boil. Then I lowered the heat to simmer. The other 3 cups of berries and ½ cup of water I put in the blender. After blending it, I added some of this mixture in a little bit at a time over the course of probably 1-2 hours of simmering. The water cooks off and makes it thick, then you add more. Let it cook down, add more mixture. Keep on doing until the other mixture is gone. Next time I make this, I might just put all the blended stuff in at once. This is just how I did it on the first try. It is delicious and reminds me of my grandma!

# Main Dishes

## Shrimp & Scallops in a Buttered Garlic Sauce (Carole)

Shrimp
2 cups rice, cooked
3 tbsp. butter
1 ½ tsp. garlic powder
6 large shrimp
6 scallops
In a frying pan melt butter and add garlic powder. Add the shrimp and scallops and fry turning once until golden brown. Set aside.

Vegetables
3 tbsp. butter
1 tsp. garlic powder
½ cup of peppers (*I use red/yellow/orange*)

½ cup chopped onions (*if can tolerate*)
½ cup sliced mushrooms
¼ cup sliced carrots
½ cup chopped broccoli
½ cup chopped cauliflower

In a frying pan, melt butter and add garlic. Add peppers, onions, mushrooms, carrots, broccoli and cauliflower. Cook until vegetables are tender. Add shrimp, scallops and rice. Mix well and heat well. Pour into serving platter or plate. In the same frying pan melt another 3 tbsp. butter and 1 tsp. garlic powder. Pour over dish. Serve and enjoy.

## Chamomile Poached Tilapia (mareng9)

2 tilapia fillets
2 bags chamomile tea
2 bay leaves
fresh ginger
salt and white pepper to taste
roasted red peppers (*optional*)

Boil two cups of water. In a heat-safe container, pour the boiling water over the tea bags. Let the tea steep for five minutes. Press a spoon against the tea bags to get as much tea out as possible. Take approximately two inches of the fresh ginger and slice it thinly. Add the bay leaves to a 12-inch skillet. In the 12-inch skillet, bring the tea and ginger to a boil over high heat. Add fillets. Reduce heat to low and simmer covered 6 minutes or until fish flakes with a fork. Remove the fillets from the liquid. Salt and pepper to taste; if desired, garnish with the roasted red peppers.

## Easy Shrimp Scampi (Bladderella)

1 lb. uncooked shrimp, peeled and deveined
3 tbsp. olive oil
3 tbsp. butter
¼ cup chicken stock (*organic, homemade, or whichever one you can tolerate*)
1 tsp. basil
1 tsp. salt
½ tsp. onion powder
1 tsp. ground black pepper (*if you can tolerate*)
2 garlic cloves, diced or 1 tsp. granulated garlic powder

12-16 oz cooked penne pasta or your favorite pasta
¼ cup chopped fresh parsley

In a large pan, heat the oil over medium heat. Add the butter (the oil will keep the butter from burning). Once the butter has melted, add the stock. Allow the sauce to come to a slight boil. Sprinkle in the basil, salt, pepper, onion powder and garlic. Toss the ingredients to mix well. Add the shrimp. They will cook quickly, about 2-3 minutes on each side. Once the shrimp have cooked, turn off the heat and place your cooked pasta into the pan with the shrimp. Sprinkle in the parsley and toss everything together and serve.

## Crispy Coconut Shrimp (Carole)

24 medium Shrimp
¾ cup Flour
½ tsp. garlic and any herb seasoning you desire
1 egg, well beaten
¼ tsp. black pepper *(if can tolerate)*
¼ cup shredded Coconut

Preheat oven to 425 degrees. Spray large baking sheet with non-stick spray. Sprinkle shrimp evenly with seasoning blend and pepper. Place the flour, egg, and coconut in three small separate bowls. Dip shrimp first in egg, then flour, then back in egg, then generously in coconut. Arrange shrimp on baking sheet. Bake 12 to 15 minutes or until golden and crisp. Serve and enjoy!

## Sinful Salmon (HRJ)

*I call this sinful because I was dairy free before dealing with IC and have had to eat some to get by. In an effort to forego the lemon you usually put on salmon, I use a LOT of butter. This is a great dish when you are tired of plain chicken and bland foods- this has a lot of flavor!*

.60 lb. of salmon filet
5-6 tbsp. butter
5 gloves of fresh, minced garlic
fresh parsley
fresh dill
a pinch or two of salt

I make a rub with the butter, garlic, parsley and salt. Let the butter come to room temperature so you can stir it all together. Use enough parsley to get bits of green throughout the butter. Grease a pan, lay the fillets in, and puts chunks of the butter all over the fillet. Then take a few springs of fresh dill and lay on top and beside the fish. Cover with foil and bake in a 350 oven for about 10-20 minutes. The fish department told me 10 minutes, but my oven takes a little longer. Keep an eye on it and don't over cook, or it will dry out. If you have a meat thermometer, it should be about 155 degrees when you take it out. I serve with a side of veggies and brown rice.

## Tuna or Salmon Burgers (Diane M)

2 cans tuna or salmon
2 slices bread *(I used potato bread or any IC friendly bread)*
1 or 2 eggs beaten

Tear the bread into small pieces in a bowl. Beat the egg and add to the bread crumbs and stir until mixed. Add the tuna and break apart any chunks with a fork, if necessary. Stir the mixture until mixed and mold into burgers. Add some milk or water if the mixture is too dry. Cook in a skillet with a little oil until they are stiff.

*\*I recommend chunk white albacore tuna in water, salt free if possible. You can drain it or not, your choice. In the end, you just want the mixture the right consistency for molding into burgers so they don't fall apart in the skillet, or in your hands for that matter. If you can't find salt free tuna, draining the water will reduce the salt content some. Great either hot or cold.*

## Baked Fish with Almond Stuffing (Diane M)

1 (5 to 6 lb.) whole bass or red snapper, cleaned and washed
¼ cup chopped onion *(if can tolerate)*
2 tbsp. butter
3 cups soft bread crumbs
½ cup chopped celery
½ cup chopped green onion *(if can tolerate)*
½ cup chopped and toasted almonds
3 eggs, lightly beaten
2 tbsp. chopped fresh parsley
1 tsp. dried tarragon

8 tbsp. butter
Salt and pepper to taste

Preheat oven to 400º. Sauté onion in 2 tbsp. butter until soft. Add bread crumbs, celery, green pepper, almonds, eggs, parsley and tarragon and mix well. Stuff cavity of fish with mixture and sew shut. Melt 8 tbsp. butter, line a large shallow baking dish with foil, and pour a little melted butter over the bottom. Place fish on the foil and sprinkle with salt and pepper. Bake for 1 hour and 15 minutes, basting frequently with remaining melted butter, or until fish flakes easily with a fork. Do not overcook.

## Salmon Loaf (Diane M)

2 cans (7 1/2 oz. each) pink salmon
1 medium onion, finely chopped (if can tolerate)
1 large stalk celery, chopped
1 tbsp. butter
½ cup quick-cooking rolled oats
¼ cup egg substitute
½ tsp. dried thyme
½ tsp. dried basil
¼ tsp. dry mustard (if can tolerate)
1/8 tsp. ground celery seeds
1/8 tsp. ground black pepper (if can tolerate)
¼ tsp. salt (optional)

Drain the salmon, reserving 3 tbsp. of the liquid and placing the liquid in a medium bowl. Remove and discard the skin from the salmon. Transfer the salmon to the bowl with the liquid. Use a fork to flake the salmon and crush the bones.

In a 2 cup glass measure, stir together the onions, celery and butter. Cover with wax paper. Microwave on high power for 2 minutes. Add the onion mixture to the salmon. Stir in the oats, eggs, thyme, basil, mustard, celery seeds, pepper and salt. Mix well.

Lightly spray an 8-inch x 4-inch glass loaf pan with no-stick spray. Transfer the salmon mixture to the dish. Lightly pat evenly in the dish. Bake at 350 F for 35 minutes. Place the pan on a wire rack and let stand for 5 minutes.

Cut the loaf into 1-inch slices and use a wide-blade spatula to remove the slices from the dish. Serves 4.

# POULTRY

## Turkey and Apple Meatloaf (wagamama)

*I "invented" this recipe after thinking about what I could use to substitute for tomato sauce in a turkey meatloaf recipe. Why not applesauce? And throw some chunks of apple in there, too? It came out really moist and my family (including my 8-year-old son) loved it. It reminds me of chicken and apple sausage. Try serving with mashed potatoes or mashed sweet potatoes.*

2 tsp. olive oil
¼ cup chopped sweet onion (optional, use if can tolerate)
1 clove garlic, chopped
1 medium Gala or similar apple, chopped coarsely
1 tsp. poultry seasoning or powdered sage
20 oz. lean ground turkey
1 large egg, beaten
½ cup dry breadcrumbs
½ tsp. salt (adjust to taste)
½ cup plus 2 tbsp. unsweetened applesauce (use a brand with no added ascorbic acid; organic usually works for me)
2 tbsp. honey

Preheat oven to 350 degrees F. Mix 2 tbsp. of unsweetened applesauce with honey in a small bowl and set aside. Heat oil over in medium skillet over medium-high heat. Add onion, garlic, chopped apple, and poultry seasoning or sage. Sauté about five minutes or until onion softens. Cool slightly. In large bowl, add turkey, egg, breadcrumbs, salt, and ½ cup of applesauce. Stir until well combined. Add apple mixture and blend. Press turkey mixture into 8" x 4" loaf pan and shape. Bake at 350 degrees F. Spoon the applesauce/honey mixture over the meatloaf after 30 minutes, and cook for a total of 45-50 minutes or until thermometer registers 165 degrees F. Let rest 10 minutes before slicing into eight portions and serving.

## Chicken Broccoli Alfredo (Bladderella)

6 oz. angel hair pasta or fettuccine
2 chicken breasts, cut in pieces
3 tbsp. olive oil
2 cups broccoli florets
¼ cup butter, melted
1 ½ cups heavy cream
¼ tsp. garlic powder
1 cup Parmesan cheese, grated
salt and pepper (*to taste*)
⅓ cup milk (optional)
¼ cup Parmesan cheese (garnish)

Cook angel hair pasta in salted water until al dente stage and drain well. Cook broccoli florets in boiling water for 3 minutes and drain. In a large sauce pan, sauté chicken pieces until done. Remove and set aside. In same pan melt butter and add cream, garlic powder, salt and pepper. Heat for 2 minutes without boiling. Add Parmesan cheese and stir to melt. Add chicken pieces, cooked pasta and broccoli florets lightly tossing to coat. If you want more sauce, use optional milk. Serve and sprinkle Parmesan cheese as a garnish. Enjoy!

## Turkey and Rice Bake (Carole)

6 slices nitrate free bacon
1 medium onion, chopped (*if can tolerate*)
¼ cup sliced onion (*if can tolerate*)
2 cups cooked rice
1 10 oz. package frozen chopped spinach or broccoli, cooked and drained
¼ tsp. salt
1 can (10 ¾ oz.) condensed cream of mushroom soup (*Make sure IC friendly. I use Amy's brand.*)
½ cup plain kefir, yogurt or sour cream (*select what you can tolerate*)
6 – 8 turkey slices
½ cup fine dry bread crumbs (*make sure IC friendly*)
1 tbsp. melted butter

Cook bacon until crisp. Drain on paper towels then crumble. In 2 tbsp. of the drippings in the same skillet, cook onion and celery until just tender. Combine the rice, bacon, onion, celery, spinach, and ¼ tsp. of salt. Combine the soup and kefir or yogurt then stir half of it into the rice and vegetable mixture. Spoon mixture into a lightly greased 11" x 7" baking dish. Arrange turkey slices over rice and vegetable mixture. Spoon remaining soup and sour cream mixture over turkey. Toss bread crumbs with butter and sprinkle around edge of casserole. Bake in a preheated 350° oven for 30 to 35 minutes, until hot and browned around the edge.

## Chinese Almond Chicken (Kadi)

3 boneless skinless chicken thighs
1 tbsp. cornstarch
1 tsp. salt
1 tsp. sugar
3 tbsp. canola oil
2 stalks celery, chopped
handful of raw almonds
garlic powder (*if you can tolerate it*)

Mix the cornstarch, sugar & salt in a mixing bowl. Rinse, then slice the chicken thighs into bite sized pieces. Put them into the cornstarch, sugar and salt mixture in the mixing bowl & stir until covered. Add the chopped celery & almonds & stir again. Heat the canola oil in a frying pan on medium-high heat, then add the chicken mix. It should sizzle a bit. Lightly sprinkle garlic across the chicken mix. Cook until chicken is done & is golden brown. Serve with white rice by itself or with steamed vegetables on the side.

*For flares: Sometimes I make this with just the chicken & without the celery, almonds & garlic. It's still tasty & is an especially good soothing recipe when flaring. And somehow, eating with chopsticks makes me feel less deprived & more "normal."*

## Light and Easy Chicken and Dumplings (Briza)

*I like this recipe because it makes a much lighter than usual chicken and dumplings. It has more of a broth rather than a creamy base. My friends always love it because it is a bit different. I'm making it today because I haven't made it all winter and I think we just got the last major cold front of the season (hopefully!)*

3-4 chicken breasts bone-in, skin removed
water
1 bay leaf

1 tsp. ground sage or poultry seasoning (*if tolerated*)
 salt and pepper (*if tolerated*)
1 cup celery, sliced
1 cup carrots, sliced
1 cup frozen peas
¼ cup fresh parsley minced (*optional*)
1 can of biscuits...like Pillsbury or Bisquick® biscuit dough (*check ingredients on these! I can tolerate them fine but some contain soy and possibly other offending ingredients*).

Put chicken in Dutch oven and cover with enough water.  Add bay leaf and sage or poultry seasoning or salt pepper. Bring to boil and boil chicken over med heat until done (20 minutes or so?). Remove chicken and let cool a bit then debone.  Add carrots and celery to the broth and cook until almost done. Reduce heat to simmer. Add peas, parsley, and deboned chicken. Tear canned biscuits into marble size pieces and drop on top of broth until entire surface is covered. (Or drop in teaspoons of Bisquick®.) Cover and simmer for 15 minutes. Don't peak or stir!

*You can use a whole chicken and remove skin after it is cooked. Whole chicken will need to cook a bit longer. Chicken thighs can also be used. I imagine you could use boneless chicken breasts but I really like the flavor that bone in chicken gives the broth.*

## Pizza Chicken (Carole)

1 boneless chicken breast, pounded flat if thick
salt & pepper (*if can tolerate*)
garlic powder and Italian seasoning, to taste
1 tbsp. nomato sauce
nitrate free sausage, slices (*make sure IC friendly*)
1 tsp. butter or oil
2 fresh mushrooms, sliced
2 thin green pepper rings (*if can tolerate otherwise use red pepper*)
1 oz. Mozzarella cheese, shredded

Season the chicken with salt and other seasonings; grill/cook. Meanwhile, sauté the mushrooms and pepper rings in butter or oil until slightly tender, but not mushy; set aside. Spread the sauce over the chicken, then top with the sausage, the pepper rings, mushrooms

and then finally, the cheese. Sprinkle with a little additional Italian seasoning, if desired. Bake at 350º about 10-15 minutes or until hot and the cheese is melted. Serve at once.

## Chicken Fajitas with Roasted Red Peppers (Bladderella)

*The filling will keep well for about 48 hours in the fridge. Reheat gently.*

1 medium white onion (*peeled and sliced thin*)
1 red bell pepper
olive oil spray
12 oz. boneless skinless chicken breast (*slice into thin strips*)
¼ tsp. salt
¼ tsp. ground cumin
¼ cup water
4 low-fat soft flour tortillas
2 tsp. non-fat sour cream (per serving) (optional)
1 tbsp. fresh cilantro leaves (per serving)

Preheat the oven to 350°F. Place the red pepper in the oven and roast for about 40 minutes. Turn the pepper a quarter turn about every ten minutes so that it roasts evenly. Remove the roasted pepper from the oven and place in a paper bag, closing the top. Allow the pepper to cool. Once cool the skin of the pepper will slip off easily. Remove the seeds and slice the pepper very thin.

Heat a large non-stick skillet over medium-high heat. Once the pan is hot, drain the onions and add them to the pan. Stir frequently. As the excess water begins to evaporate, spray lightly with the olive oil. Continue to cook until the onions are completely brown. If they cook too fast, reduce the heat to keep them from burning. When the onions are well browned and limp, add the sliced roasted red bell pepper. Stir and increase the heat to medium-high and add the chicken, salt and cumin. Cook until the outside of the chicken strips are slightly browned.

Place a second skillet on another burner over high heat. Add the water to the pan with the chicken mixture and cook, stirring frequently.

The water will evaporate quickly and when there is only about a tbsp. left, remove the pan from the burner.

Place a tortilla in the second heated pan for about 5 – 10 seconds, turning once so that the tortilla is soft. Remove and fill with ¼ of the fajita mixture, top with 2 tsp. non-fat sour cream *(optional)* and 1 tbsp. cilantro leaves. Repeat for the other three fajitas and serve.

*\*To reduce the "burn" of the onion, you can place the sliced onion in a large mixing bowl and cover with the water and ice.*

## Chicken Casserole (Diane M)
3 cups cooked chicken (cut up)
1 can cream of chicken soup(IC friendly or could use cream of mushroom)
1 1/2 cup cooked rice
1 cup chopped celery
2 small packages of slivered almonds
1 cup chicken broth(IC friendly)
2 hard-boiled eggs chopped

Mix all ingredients in a large casserole. Cover with 2 cups of crushed Cornflakes (make sure IC friendly). Bake in 350-degree oven for 1 hour or until bubbling around the edges.

## Low Fat IC Friendly Turkey Meatloaf (CBZ1982)

*This is my own recipe. I decided to use ingredients that I knew wouldn't bother my IC.*

1 lb. ground turkey
8 saltine crackers or your favorite bread crumbs
1 egg
garlic salt *(however much you want)*
kosher salt or regular table salt *(however much you want)*
Mozzarella cheese, shredded *(however much you want)*

Crumble the crackers into the mixture the order in which you add the ingredients doesn't matter. Mix by hand until everything is mixed in. Cook at 375 degrees until the meat is cooked thoroughly.

## BBQ Chicken (Carole)
*I explored with my barbecue sauce recipe and made this chicken. I really enjoyed it. It has lots of flavor and makes me feel like I'm cheating.*

In a casserole dish lay chicken in the bottom. You can use any kind of chicken you want. Pour BBQ sauce over chicken. Recipe below. Bake at 350 degrees for 45-50 minutes. You can even pour the sauce over rice or on top of a baked potato.

BBQ Sauce Large Portion Recipe
1 small can yam puree
1 small can beets
1 can pears rinsed and drained
1 cup pear juice
3 roasted red peppers *(see note below)*
½ cup corn syrup
½ cup brown sugar
1 tsp. allspice *(if you can tolerate I can't so I don't use it)*
1 large clove garlic crushed
¼ cup chopped onions *(if can tolerate otherwise use chives)*
¼ cup unsulfured molasses

In medium pot mix together the above ingredients and simmer on low until flavors merry approx 30 minutes. Stir often.

BBQ Sauce small Portion Recipe (good for 2-4 breasts):
I cup basic Nomato Sauce
¼ cup corn syrup
¼ cup brown sugar
1 large crushed garlic clove
¼ chopped onion *(if can tolerate otherwise use chives)*
1 tbsp. unsulfured molasses
½ tsp. allspice *(if can tolerate)*

In small pot mix the above ingredients and simmer.

**Note:** *Roasting Red Peppers. Clean and cut peppers in half. Rub generously with olive oil. Add seasoning (use generous amounts). You can use any you want. I use garlic, basil, thyme, pepper, oregano and sea salt. Bake in oven at 450 degrees until tender. Cool and peel skin off.*

## Grilled Chicken with Cucumber Yogurt Sauce (Raiinboweyes)

1 6 oz. carton plain low-fat yogurt (*greek nonfat yogurt recommended*)
¼ cup thinly sliced green onions
2 tsp. to 1 tbsp. snipped fresh mint, chopped
½ tsp. ground cumin (*if tolerated*)
¼ tsp. salt
1/8 tsp. ground black pepper (*if tolerated*)
1 cup chopped, seeded cucumber
4 small skinless, boneless chicken breast halves (*1 to 1¼ pounds total*)
1/8 tsp. ground black pepper (*if tolerated*)

In a medium bowl, combine yogurt, green onions, mint, cumin (if tolerated), salt, and 1/8 tsp. pepper (if tolerated). Transfer half of the yogurt mixture to a small bowl; set aside. For cucumber-yogurt sauce: Stir cucumber into remaining yogurt mixture.

Sprinkle chicken breasts with 1/8 tsp. pepper. Place chicken on the rack of an uncovered grill directly over medium coals. Grill for 12 to 15 minutes or until chicken is no longer pink (170 degrees F), turning once halfway through grilling and brushing with reserved yogurt mixture for the last half of grilling. Discard any remaining yogurt mixture. Serve chicken with the cucumber-yogurt sauce.

*Tip: If you can't tolerate green onions, or just don't have them, 2 tbsp. of dried chives and a 1-2 pinches of onion powder works wonderfully as a substitute!*

## White Chicken Chili (mrmambo)

*This is something I make for my wife from time to time... and this seemed like a good time!*

3 lb. bone-in, skin-on chicken breast halves, trimmed of excess fat and skin
1 tbsp. vegetable oil
1 lb. red bell pepper
2 cups medium onions, cut into large pieces (*or leeks, if sensitive*)
6 medium cloves garlic, minced or pressed through garlic press (about 2 tbsp.)
1 tbsp. ground cumin (*or half caraway/half anise seeds, ground*)
1 ½ tsp. ground coriander

2 (14.5 oz.) cans white cannellini beans, drained and rinsed
3 cups low-sodium chicken broth
½ tsp. lemon extract, to taste (*optional. Lemon peel is less acidic*)
¼ cups minced fresh cilantro leaves (*optional*)
4 scallions or leeks, sliced thin

Season chicken liberally with salt and pepper. Heat oil in large Dutch oven over medium-high heat until just smoking. Add chicken, skin side down, and cook without moving until skin is golden brown, about 4 minutes. Using tongs, turn chicken and lightly brown on other side, about 2 minutes. Transfer chicken to plate; remove and discard skin.

While chicken is browning, remove and discard ribs and seeds from bell peppers. In food processor, process half of peppers and onions until consistency of chunky salsa, ten to twelve 1-second pulses, scraping down sides of food processor halfway through. Transfer mixture to medium bowl. Repeat with remaining peppers and onions; combine with first batch (do not wash food processor blade or workbowl).

Pour off all but 1 tbsp. fat from Dutch oven (adding additional vegetable oil if necessary) and reduce heat to medium. Add pepper-onion mixture, garlic, cumin, coriander, and ¼ tsp. salt. Cover and cook, stirring occasionally, until vegetables soften, about 10 minutes. Remove pot from heat.

Transfer 1 cup cooked vegetable mixture to now-empty food processor workbowl. Add 1 cup beans and 1 cup broth and process until smooth, about 20 seconds. Add vegetable-bean mixture, remaining 2 cups broth, and chicken breasts to Dutch oven and bring to boil over medium-high heat. Reduce heat to medium-low and simmer, covered, stirring occasionally, until chicken registers 160°F (175°F if using thighs) on instant-read thermometer, 15 to 20 minutes (40 minutes if using thighs).

Using tongs, transfer chicken to large plate. Stir in remaining beans and continue to simmer, uncovered, until beans are heated through and chili has thickened slightly, about 10 minutes.

When cool enough to handle, shred chicken into bite-sized pieces, discarding bones. Stir shredded chicken, lemon extract or peel, cilantro, scallions into chili and return to simmer. Adjust seasonings with salt and pepper and serve.

### Chicken Fricassee (Diane M)

3 lb. chicken pieces
flour
non-stick cooking spray
3 cups chicken broth
1 lb. baby carrots
1 tbsp. Butter
3 tbsp. flour
¾ cup milk
3 tbsp. fresh or 2 tsp. dried dill
1 tsp. sugar
½ tsp. salt

Coat chicken with flour. Spray skillet with cooking spray. Cook until brown. Drain fat. Add chicken broth. Simmer, covered, about 1 hour or until chicken is no longer pink in center. Add carrots last 20 minutes of cooking. Transfer chicken and carrots to platter keep warm. Melt butter, add flour. Cook and stir for 1 to 2 minutes. Add to chicken broth, stir in milk, dill sugar and salt. Pour over chicken. Serve with cooked noodles.

### Portobella Mushroom Chicken (valkay18)

*I made this last night, and it was SOOOO good. Tasted like I had eaten out at an expensive restaurant! It's basically breaded chicken in a bed of portabello mushrooms with a cream sauce. The chicken is smothered with Mozzarella cheese and more mushrooms.*

3 cups sliced Portabello mushrooms
4 skinless chicken breast halves
2 eggs beaten
egg noodles (*or the kind of noodles of your choosing*)
1 cup seasoned bread crumbs
2 tbsp. butter
6 oz. Mozzarella cheese

1 cup mushroom broth (*I used the "Pacific Natural Foods" Brand*)
½ block cream cheese
spices if making bread crumbs: garlic, basil, salt, oregano

Preheat oven to 350 degrees. Place half of the mushrooms in a 9" x 13" baking pan. Dip chicken into beaten eggs, and then roll in bread crumbs. In skillet, melt butter over medium heat. Brown both sides of the chicken in skillet. Place chicken on top of mushrooms.

Combine cream cheese and mushroom broth in sauce pan, and simmer & stir until cream sauce is formed. Pour sauce into the baking pan, and bake!! After about 20 minutes, add remaining mushrooms to the top of the chicken breasts, and smother in Mozzarella cheese. Total cooking time is usually 30 - 35 minutes for smaller chicken breasts. If larger ones, it may take longer.

Boil noodles. When noodles and chicken are done, serve chicken, mushrooms, and sauce over noodles.

*When I made this recipe, I made my own bread crumbs with white bread, and added garlic powder, basil, oregano, and salt. This made it taste awesome. I then added basil to the top of the mixture when I added the Mozzarella and mushrooms at the end.*

### Quinoa Pilaf with Chicken (Carole)

2 tbsp. coconut oil
1 small onion, diced (*if can tolerate*)
1 stalk celery, diced
3 carrots, diced
1 cup quinoa (*rinsed*)
2 cups chicken broth (*IC friendly*)
season to taste (*basil,sage,oregano etc..*)
1 cup shredded cooked chicken meat
salt and black pepper (*to taste or tolerance*)

Heat the coconut oil in a saucepan over medium heat. Cook and stir the onion, celery, and carrots in the hot oil until tender, about 7 minutes. Add the quinoa, chicken broth, seasoning. Bring to a boil over high heat. Reduce heat to medium-low, cover, and simmer until the liquid has been absorbed and the quinoa is tender, about 20 minutes. Stir in the chicken season with salt and pepper.

*Note can add shredded coconut after cooking to give a sweeter flavor and add some more texture.*

## Yummy Chicken (just1ofamillion)

Take a thawed chicken breast and cut it in half across the width. Then cut a pocket into the chicken halves and fill this with spinach and feta cheese. Sometimes I need to put a couple of toothpicks in to help it all stay in the chicken. Then season however you like. I like salt, garlic, and rosemary. Then I use a George Foreman Grill and cook for about 10 minutes. It's quick, easy, and not very expensive. Oh, and IC friendly.

## Chicken & Veggie Kebabs (Kadi)

Using a bamboo skewer, pierce small pieces of chicken, zucchini "coins", mushroom halves, red bell pepper slices & cook them on the George Foreman grill. For flavor, I mixed canola oil with a little basil, oregano, garlic powder, salt & tossed the pieces in this before cooking. Serve over brown rice & add ½ tbsp. of Marie's Lite Creamy ranch dressing on the side to dip your fork in before bites.

*Trader Joe's makes a great brown rice you keep in the freezer & microwave for 3 minutes, Voila! Brown rice without the wait.*

## BEEF

### Stuffed Meatloaf (Carole)

Meatloaf:
In large bowl assemble the ingredients below then set aside
1 ½ lbs. of ground beef
1 egg
⅔ cup IC friendly bread crumbs
¼ cup milk
½ tsp. garlic
½ tsp. oregano
½ tsp. basil
½ tsp. thyme
½ tsp. black pepper
1 small chopped onion or chives (if can tolerate)

Filling:
In a medium bowl assemble the ingredients below
3 cups sliced mushrooms
1 tbsp. butter
3 tbsp. flour
1/2 a block of cream cheese cut into chunks

Blend all above ingredients together then take ⅔ of the mixture and mold into the loaf pan. Make a tunnel down the center like a hollow log. Fill the hollow center with the filling spreading evenly. Add remaining meat mixture on top making sure center is well sealed. Bake at 350 for 1hr. Let cool slightly then cut and serve.

## Beef Hash & Cabbage (cgoheen)

*I had some left over pot roast and my wife wanted me to learn how to make beef hash and cabbage. This is what I threw together last night. Turned out pretty well so I thought I would share.*

Cut pot roast into ¼" cubes. You can also finely shred the beef.
Cut 3 medium potatoes into ¼" cubes (I prefer Yukon Gold.)
½ head of cabbage shredded (1" x 1" inch chunks or smaller depending on preference)
Seasonings as preferred.

In a large skillet, heat 1 tbsp. of butter and ½ tbsp. of olive oil. Add potatoes and coat them with the oil. Cover the bottom of the pan with hot water ( ½ - ¾ of a cup). Season potatoes. I used a generous amount of garlic salt. Layer beef on top of potatoes. Add cabbage to the top of that. At this point, I added a little kosher salt to the cabbage. Bring the water to a boil. Lower heat, cover, and simmer for 10 minutes or until potatoes are tender. Remove the cover, stir everything together, and brown over medium heat. Turn once, brown some more and server.

## Sizzling Steaks with Toasted Garlic Sauce (Diane M)

4 lean steaks *(about 5 oz. each)*
ground or fresh basil

ground or fresh rosemary
1 tbsp. olive oil
5 cloves garlic, minced
½ cup beef broth *(IC friendly)*
1 tbsp. butter

Season steaks with basil and rosemary. Heat oil in a skillet over medium-high heat. Add steaks. Cook until desired doneness (about 4 minutes per side for medium rare). Remove from pan and cover to keep warm. Add garlic and sauté until golden, about 2 minutes. Add broth. Scrape to remove any browned bits stuck to the bottom of the pan and cook to reduce by half, about 4 minutes. Add butter, mix well, and pour over steaks.

## Beef Rib Eye Roast w/ Potatoes, Mushrooms, and Fancy Pan Gravy (Diane M)

1 tbsp. chopped fresh rosemary leaves
2 garlic cloves, minced
2 tsp. kosher salt
1 tsp. freshly ground black pepper *(if can tolerate)*
1 beef rib eye roast *(about 4 lbs.)*
1 tbsp. vegetable oil
4 lbs. small new potatoes, cut in half
1 lbs. large white mushrooms, quartered
1 tbsp. butter, softened
1 tbsp. flour
1 (14-½ oz.) can beef broth *(low sodium)*

Preheat oven to 350F. In a small bowl mix together the rosemary, garlic, salt, and pepper. Spread evenly over the surface of the roast. Place roast, fat-side-up on a rack in a shallow roasting pan. Insert a meat thermometer into the center of the roast. Place pan in the center of the oven, and cook for 40 minutes. Remove pan from oven. Toss potatoes with oil and add to the pan, stir to coat with the juices, and season with salt and pepper.

Return pan to oven and continue to cook for 20 minutes. Add the mushrooms, stir to coat, and continue cooking for 40 more minutes. Mix together the butter and flour and set aside. Remove roast (thermometer should read 130F) to a cutting surface and let sit 15 minutes

before carving. Place vegetables on a serving platter. Pour the pan juices into a small saucepan and skim off the fat. Add the additional beef broth, bring to a boil and let cook for 3 minutes. Lower the heat, add the butter and flour mixture and whisk carefully to incorporate. Carve beef and serve with gravy, mushrooms, and potatoes.

## Flank Steak and Roasted Cauliflower with Yogurt and Cilantro (rawestrus)

*This meal works better for those who can eat foods on the "try it" list. I'll flag anything questionable. Really easy prep.*

Roasted cauliflower:
Preheat oven to 400 F. Take one head of cauliflower, cutting it into florets. In a casserole dish or just a baking pan lined with aluminum foil, spread out evenly. Drizzle all pieces with olive oil and sprinkle some thinly sliced garlic cloves likewise. Add some salt. Then place in oven for 30 minutes. At about the 20 minute mark, get to work on the meat.

Steak:
I had some flank steak and thinly sliced it across the grain - enough for one portion for myself. Sprinkled a little salt and pepper onto the meat.

I diced one small shallot. Cut two cubes of unsalted butter. Heat up a skillet until it's nice and hot, add butter, shallots, then within ONE MINUTE or less just toss in the beef, see that it gets brown on the outside with maybe a hint of pink poking through and then immediately dish onto a plate and get it out of that pan! (That's if you like it tender and a bit rare). Let it stand.

Take out your cauliflower from the oven, and add as many pieces as you like to your plate. Pour plain yogurt over top (I like organic Balkan style yogurt but I think I will try goat yogurt in the future since I might tolerate it better) and sprinkle chopped cilantro generously. The yogurt and cilantro make it nice and almost tangy. I previously tried this roasted cauliflower with Parmesan sprinkled on top and felt like it fell flat a bit just with

Parmesan. Ingredients you may not be able to tolerate: shallots, yogurt, cilantro. This filled me up and felt sort of comforting.

## Shepherd's Pie with Homemade Cream Corn (Carole)

Bottom Layer (meat layer):
*1 small package ground beef* (approx 1/2-2lbs)
½ tsp. pepper (if can tolerate)
½ tsp. garlic powder
¼ tsp. sea salt
Brown ground beef in frying pan until cooked. Drain and add seasoning. Set aside.

Middle Layer (potato layer):
6 large potatoes
3 tbsp. butter
½ cup of milk
Boil the potatoes until tender and then drain. In a large mixing bowl with an electric mixer blend potatoes with butter and milk until smooth. Set aside

Top Layer (cream corn layer):
500g bag of frozen corn (approx. 4 cups)
3 tbsp. of butter
1 ½ cups of whipping cream
3 tbsp. of sugar
2 tsp. of cornstarch
Mix all the above ingredients in a medium sauce pan. Boil lightly until mixture thickens. Pour into blender and just give about a 5-10 second blend.

Assembly:
In a medium casserole dish spread meat layer on the bottom, then add the potato layer and finishing with the cream corn layer. Bake at 300 in the over for 30 minutes or until heated through.

# PORK

## Stuffed Pork Chops (Carole)

*Seen a version of this on a cooking show. I have modified the recipe to make it IC friendly. Makes 4 stuffed pork chops.*

4 nitrate free sausage without the casing.

1 ½ tbsp. of fresh sage chopped.
1 cup of your favorite cheese (*Monterey Jack if you can tolerate*)
2 chopped peaches or apples
4 boneless pork chops

Place the sausage in a frying pan with a little olive oil and fry.  In a bowl add sage, cheese and peaches or apples. Add sausage and mix together.

Cut pockets in the pork chops (butterfly like) but do not cut all the way through. Stuff each pork chops with the sausage mixture. Use a skewer that was soaked in water to hold shut each chop. Pan fry in a little olive oil to brown each side. Transfer to a covered casserole dish and cook at 400 degrees for 25 minutes.

## Sausage and Potato Foil Packet (Carole)

4 nitrate free sausage links, uncooked
8 potatoes
1 cup fresh green beans, ends cut
olive oil or butter
1 garlic clove, minced
salt & pepper to taste and tolerance

Cut potatoes, beans and sausage into bite size pieces. In a foil packet, combine sausage, potatoes and green beans. Add spices and drizzle oil on top or put dollops of butter. Close your foil packet and wrap a second time. Bake at 415 degrees for 30 minutes.

## Pork Loin in the Crockpot with Butternut Squash (HRJ)

2 small pork loins
rosemary, garlic and salt
butternut squash cut in chunks (Trader Joes sells it in a bag already cut up)
olive oil, butter, or ghee

Top the pork with rosemary, salt, and garlic. Sauté the butternut squash with some butter, ghee, olive oil and salt. This gets some of the water out of it, so it isn't too watery in the crockpot. Brown the edges. Add the squash around the pork loin. Drizzle with olive oil. Cook on high for 4 hours or low for longer.

### Maple Encrusted Pork Chops (Carole)

Coat as many pork chops as you would like with the following:

bowl one: flour
bowl two: beaten egg
bowl three: bread crumbs, 2-3 tbsp. maple syrup, any seasoning you would like (I use "simply organic" powdered ranch and creamy dill. You could use rosemary, dill, thyme, garlic.) You can also add Parmesan if you can tolerate. Mix the maple syrup through. It will be sticky but it will adhere to the pork chop.

Spread a thin layer of cream cheese on both sides of the pork chop (I use Boursin Garlic and fine herbs but just plain cream cheese is fine.) Starting from bowl one and ending in bowl three, dip pork chop in each bowl coating both sides. You will have to press on the breadcrumb mixture.

Place on cookie sheet covered in foil. Bake at 350 for about 45 minutes. Cooking time depends on size of the pork chops.

### Easter Ham (Carole)

4-6 Gala apples, sliced
1½ - 2 cups brown sugar
2-3 cups pear juice
2 tbsp. flour or cornstarch
2 tbsp. corn syrup

I slice my ham into slices and lay it in a pan. I then combine all the above ingredients and pour over ham slices. I cover pan with foil and put the lid over the foil. I slow cook it at 300 degrees until it carmelizes. I cook it for about 2 ½ to 3 hours.

*Measurements vary depending on how big your ham is. Increase recipe as needed. Sorry but my measurement are approximate as I usually just throw stuff in. You can also add a little maple syrup if you desire. See Raisin Sauce recipe for Carole's glaze!*

### Pork Chops with Pears or Apples (Briza)

*This makes really tasty tender pork chops. Served with white rice is great with the juice poured over.*

2 tbsp. olive oil

1 onion, sliced *(optional)*
2 cloves garlic *(optional)*
4-6 pork chops
12 oz. pear or apple juice or nectar
1 pear or apple sliced *(you can also use dried pears or apples if they don't contain preservatives)*

Heat oil in a skillet over medium heat. Cook onion and garlic until just turning brown. Push onion and garlic to sides of pan and brown pork chops on both sides. Add pears or apples. Add juice, cover and simmer over low heat at least 30 minutes. The longer it cooks the more tender.

## VEGETARIAN

### Zucchini Rice Gratin (mareng9)

*I like to make this for supper. Leave out the onions if they bother you! I adapted this from a favorite recipe of mine that had roasted tomatoes. I substituted roasted red bell peppers instead. Just be sure to taste the rice mixture before you add the eggs. It may need just an extra bit of seasoning.*

⅓ cup uncooked white rice
4 tbsp. olive oil
1 ½ pounds zucchini (about 3 medium), sliced 1/4-inch thick
½ pound roasted red peppers, chopped into bite-sized pieces
table salt and white pepper
1 medium onion, halved lengthwise and thinly sliced
1 ½ tsp. of garlic powder *(if tolerated)*
2 large eggs, lightly beaten
1 tsp. chopped fresh thyme leaves
½ cup grated Parmesan, divided

Preheat oven to 450°F. Cook the rice. While rice cooks, coat one large baking sheet with a tbsp. of olive oil (a bit less for smaller pans). Spread zucchini slices on the baking sheets in as close to a single layer as you can. Sprinkle with ½ tsp. salt and a few grinds of white pepper. Roast the zucchini for 20 minutes. Flip zucchini halfway through.

Heat large, heavy skillet over medium heat. Once hot, add 2 tbsp. olive oil, heat oil, then add onions, garlic and ¼ tsp. salt to pan. Cover and reduce heat to low, cooking onion until limp and tender, about 15 to 20 minutes. Stir occasionally.

Taste bits of your dish to see if you have enough seasoning. Combine onion mixture, rice, eggs, thyme, half of your grated cheese and a ½ tbsp. of olive oil in a bowl. Add a good amount of white pepper. Use the remaining ½ tbsp. of olive oil to coat a shallow 2 quart baking dish. Spread half of the rice mixture in bottom of dish. Arrange half of roasted zucchini on top. Spread remaining rice mixture over it. Arrange remaining zucchini on top, then the roasted red pepper slices. Sprinkle with remaining grated cheese and bake until set and golden brown, about 20 minutes.

## Vegetarian Shepherds Pie (agilityme)

6 - 7 medium russet potatoes, cut in thirds
almond milk, regular milk or cream
3 large carrots, sliced on the diagonal
½ small head of cauliflower (cut into small florets)
1 small head of broccoli (cut into small florets)
1 cup frozen peas
splash olive oil
salt and pepper to taste (if tolerated)
mushroom gravy (see recipe in sauce section)

Boil russet potatoes in salted water until tender. Drain and mash with either almond milk, regular milk or cream. Don't add too much liquid - soupy mashed potatoes won't work well with this recipe. Stir-fry carrots, cauliflower and broccoli in large pan until crisp tender. Add frozen peas, continue to heat until peas are hot. Season with a little salt and pepper. Add all the mushrooms and enough mushroom gravy to coat the stir fried vegetables. Spoon them into a greased casserole dish. Top with mashed potatoes and bake at 350 for 30 minutes. Serve topped with remaining mushroom gravy.

Mushroom Gravy
8 oz. Baby Bella mushrooms, sliced
2 cups roasted vegetable stock (See recipe in soup section)
2 tbsp. butter or olive oil
2 tbsp. cornstarch
salt to taste
pepper to taste (if tolerated)

Coat large pan with either olive oil or butter. Add a single layer of sliced mushrooms. Brown one side, flip and brown the other side. Be sure not to crowd the pan or your mushrooms will not brown. It is better to do two batches than to crowd the pan. Add more butter or oil as needed. Set browned mushrooms aside. Pour cold roasted vegetable stock into a medium sized pan. Whisk in the cornstarch. Bring to a boil stiffing constantly. Reduce heat, continue to stir, add mushrooms and simmer until thickens.

## Red Beans and Rice (Briza)

1 lb. small red beans, rinsed and sorted
2 quarts water
1 onion, chopped
4 cloves garlic, minced
2 stalks celery, chopped
1 bay leaf
1 tbsp dried oregano
salt to taste

Place beans, ½ chopped onion, bay leaf, and 2 cloves minced garlic in soup pot and cover with 2 quarts or more of water. Bring to boil over medium-high heat, then reduce heat to a low boil. Cover beans with lid placed slightly askew to let steam out. Meanwhile, heat olive oil in separate pan and sauté ½ chopped onion, 2 cloves minced garlic, and chopped celery until soft.

When beans are almost done add sautéed veggies and oregano and then cover beans securely with lid. Continue cooking until beans are done. Total cooking time will be anywhere from 1.5 to 3 hours. Keep an eye on the liquid and add more while cooking if you like a soupier mix. Red beans make a nice thick gravy so I usually let most of the water cook off, which will happen if you place the lid askew for majority of the cooking time. I haven't found it necessary to pre-soak red beans. Serve with white or brown rice and cornbread.

## Mushroom Rice Medley (Diane M)

2 cups brown rice
2 cans (32 oz.) chicken broth *(IC friendly)*
8 oz. mixed fresh mushrooms *(button, shitake, cremini, etc.)*
½ cup unsalted pecans *(if can tolerate or use almonds )*
1 tbsp. olive oil
salt & pepper to taste *(if can tolerate)*

Heat chicken broth to boiling in a large saucepan. Add rice and cook according to package directions, until tender and all of the broth is absorbed, about 45 minutes. Meanwhile, chop pecans and then set aside.

Slice mushrooms into strips. Heat olive oil in a saucepan until hot but not smokings. Add mushrooms and nuts and cook until mushrooms are lightly browned. Combine hot cooked rice with mushroom mixture, season to taste with salt and pepper and serve immediately.

Put the pasta back into the warm pan and toss in olive oil, cooked sausage, parsley and half of the Parmesan cheese. Toss thoroughly. If it needs more moisture, add a bit more olive oil. Add salt and pepper to taste. Serve piping hot, topped with the remaining Parmesan cheese. Serve with a salad and French bread.

*My sister also adds a few beaten eggs then cooks slowly over medium heat so that it's more moist!*

## Macaroni and Cheese (Carole)

2 cans evaporated milk
1 cup IC friendly chicken broth
3 tbsp. butter
⅓ cup flour
½ cup grated Parmesan cheese *(if can tolerate)*
Freshly ground black pepper *(if can tolerate)*
1 pound grated Cheddar *(sharp is best but as tolerated)*

Cook your pasta and drain. Microwave milk and chicken broth until hot but not boiling. Melt butter in a medium saucepan. Whisk in flour, then hot milk mixture. Continue to whisk until thick and bubbly, 3 to 4 minutes. Whisk Parmesan and pepper. Turn off heat, stir in Cheddar until melted. Add drained pasta to sauce, and stir until everything is well combined over low heat. Heat through. Thin with a little water if too thick. Serve hot.

## White Cheese Chicken Lasagna (Carole)

*Thick with an abundance of Mozzarella, Parmesan and ricotta cheeses, this chicken and spinach lasagna could make you forget all about the tomato kind!*

9 lasagna noodles
½ cup butter
1 onion, chopped *(if can tolerate)*
1 clove garlic, minced
½ cup all-purpose flour
1 tsp. salt
2 cups chicken broth, low sodium
1 ½ cups milk
4 cups shredded Mozzarella cheese, divided
1 cup grated Parmesan cheese, divided *(if can tolerate)*
1 tsp. dried basil

# Pasta

## Carbonara Pasta (icnmgrjill)

*If you miss pasta, you must try this fabulous recipe that I adapted from a very old Sunset Italian cookbook to be more IC friendly.*

½ lb. bulk mild Italian sausage
¼ lb. ham or Canadian bacon chopped *(can easily leave this out)*
½ cup fresh mushrooms
½ cup finely chopped fresh parsley
1 cup grated or shredded Parmesan cheese
1 tbsp. olive oil *(optional)*
1 package angel hair pasta *(I prefer quinoa pasta)*
salt & pepper to taste *(optional)*

Brown ½ pound of mild Italian sausage, breaking it up into smaller, bite size bits. As it's cooking, add ham and mushrooms until well browned. At the same time, cook the pasta, drain and then place back until the warm pot.

1 tsp. dried oregano
½ tsp. ground black pepper
2 cups ricotta cheese
2 cups cubed, cooked chicken meat
2 (10 oz.) packages frozen chopped spinach, thawed and drained
1 tbsp. chopped fresh parsley
¼ cup grated Parmesan cheese for topping (if can tolerate)

Preheat oven to 350 degrees F (175 degrees C). Bring a large pot of lightly salted water to a boil. Cook lasagna noodles in boiling water for 8 to 10 minutes. Drain, and rinse with cold water.

Melt the butter in a large saucepan over medium heat. Cook the onion and garlic in the butter until tender, stirring frequently. Stir in the flour and salt, simmer until bubbly. Mix in the broth and milk, and boil, stirring constantly, for 1 minute. Stir in 2 cups Mozzarella cheese and 1/4 cup Parmesan cheese. Season with the basil, oregano, and ground black pepper. Remove from heat, and set aside.

Spread ⅓ of the sauce mixture in the bottom of a 9" x13" baking dish. Layer with ⅓ of the noodles, the ricotta, and the chicken. Arrange ⅓ of the noodles over the chicken, and layer with ⅓ of the sauce mixture, spinach, and the remaining 2 cups Mozzarella cheese and 1/2 cup Parmesan cheese. Arrange remaining noodles over cheese, and spread remaining sauce evenly over noodles. Sprinkle with parsley and ¼ cup Parmesan cheese. Bake 35 to 40 minutes in the preheated oven.

## Tomatoless Spaghetti (Dawn Grace)

2 cans 15 oz. beets, drained
1 can 30 oz. yams, drained
1 tsp. lemon oil (if IC friendly)
1 tsp. garlic salt
1 tsp. sugar
2 tsp. Italian spices
1 lb. MSG & nitrate free Sausage
1 small chopped onion
Mozzarella cheese

Puree beets and yams. Fry sausage and onion until done. Add all together in saucepan and simmer 15-20 min. Add a little water to thin. Serve over cooked spaghetti with melted Mozzarella cheese on top.

## Chicken Spaghetti (Carole)

1 whole chicken, cut up
spaghetti noodles, about half a package
1 onion, diced (if can tolerate)
1 red pepper, chopped
1 green bell pepper, chopped (if can tolerate)
2 cans cream of mushroom soup, low sodium
salt and pepper to taste
2 cups shredded Cheddar cheese plus extra for top of dish

In a large pot filled with water, boil one whole cut up chicken. Bring to boil and reduce. Cook for 25 minutes. Take chicken out. Remove 2 cups of chicken broth from the pot and set aside. Break noodles in four sections and cook in pot of broth that you cooked the chicken in. Shred chicken by hand and place in a large bowl. Add onion, red pepper and green bell pepper.

Add 2 cans of cream of mushroom soup. Add salt and pepper to taste. Add the cooked spaghetti and mix everything together. Add 1 cup of the reserved broth. Add 2 cups of shredded Cheddar. You can add more broth at this point it not liquid enough. Keep in mind that some liquid will evaporate and be absorbed during cooking. Pour all into a casserole dish. Add more shredded cheese on top. Bake 350 degrees for 35-40minutes.

## Cheesy Bacon, Chicken & Spaghetti Casserole (Carole)

4 boneless, skinless chicken breasts
4 slices nitrate free bacon
1 cup onion, diced (if can tolerate)
3 tbsp. flour
3 tbsp. butter
1 tsp. kosher salt
¼ tsp. pepper
3 cups IC friendly chicken broth
1 cup heavy cream
1 cup white cheddar cheese, grated

46

¼ cup chopped scallions
1 pound spaghetti (I used gluten free)

Season chicken breasts with salt and pepper. Cook bacon until crisp, remove from pan and chop up for later. Drain off all but 2 tbsp. of the fat. Heat pan to medium-high heat. Cook chicken in the bacon fat until well browned. You don't have to cook the chicken through. Remove chicken from pan and place in casserole dish. Drain off the bacon fat from the pan and add 3 tbsp. of butter. Once melted, stir in the onion. Cook until soft and starting to caramelize- 5-7 minutes. Stir 3 tbsp. of flour into the onions & cook for 1 minute. Stir broth and cream into the flour mixture, bring to boil - constantly stirring- for a few minutes to reduce a bit. Remove from heat. Stir in salt, pepper, cheese and pour over the chicken in the casserole dish. Bake at 350F, uncovered for 20-25 minutes or until the sauce is bubbly and chicken is cooked through. While the chicken is baking, cook 1 lb. spaghetti and drain. Remove chicken from the oven, stir pasta into the sauce and serve topped with crumbled bacon and scallions.

## Shrimp Pasta in a Cream Sauce (Diane M)

1 ½ heaping handfuls of cooked baby shrimp
1 pint heavy whipping cream
3 tbsp. of olive oil
¼ cup IC friendly chicken broth
3-5 cloves garlic
1 onion-medium sized (if can tolerate)
1 ½ tbsp. dried dill
your favorite pasta

Sauté minced garlic and chopped onion in olive oil over medium heat until garlic is lightly browned. Pour chicken broth and reduce until all the liquid is gone. Pour in the heavy whipping cream and simmer until cream thickens (about 20 minutes). Once sauce thickens, add in the shrimp and dill, cook until shrimp in hot all the way through (about 4 minutes). Serve over your favorite pasta. Serves about 4-5.

## Spinach Fettuccine (Diane M)

¼ lb fresh parsley or basil, chopped
1-2 cloves garlic, chopped
¼ c extra virgin olive oil
1 lb. spinach fettuccine noodles

Bring water to a boil, add pasta and cook until al dente. Heat the oil and garlic over medium heat.  After 2-3 minutes, add the herb. Add oil and toss thoroughly. Serve with freshly grated Parmesan cheese and a salad on side.

## Risotto w/Lobster, Chicken or Shrimp (Diane M)

2 cups arborio rice
5 cups chicken stock
½ cup onion, chopped (if can tolerate)
5 tbsp. butter
2 tbsp. vegetable oil
pinch of salt
¼ cup green onion or chives, minced
1 cup sliced lobster or chicken (cooked) or whole cleaned medium shrimp (raw)
1 pinch fresh chopped parsley

In a large saucepan, bring the chicken stock to a very slow, steady simmer.  In another large saucepan, place three tbsp. of the butter, vegetable oil and chopped onion and cook over medium heat until onion becomes translucent. Add the rice, stirring until all the grains are coated. Add ½ cup of the simmering stock and cook, stirring constantly until all of the liquid is absorbed. Be sure to stir the bottom of the pan frequently to clean off any rice mixture that may stick. Add another ½ cup of the broth and continue stirring, as above, until all liquid is absorbed. Continue adding stock, ½ cup at a time, until all is incorporated. Simmer over low heat for ten minutes, stirring constantly.

Add the meat of your choice and stir well until cooked thoroughly. Just before serving, add the remaining 2 tbsp. of butter and stir thoroughly.

## Garden Primavera Pasta (Diane M)

1 lb. mixed, precut vegetables, frozen or fresh
½ lb. angel hair pasta
1 cup shredded Mozzarella cheese

1 tbsp. olive oil
1 tsp. garlic salt

Bring a large pot of salted water to a boil. Add vegetables and cook until almost crisp tender, about 5 minutes. Add pasta and cook another 3 minutes. Drain, put back in pot and mix with remaining ingredients. Serve immediately.

## Linguine with Ricotta, Eggplant & Basil (Diane M)

½ cup olive oil
½ cup eggplant: peeled, salted, and drained
¼ tsp. garlic, chopped
½ sweet red pepper
4 oz. fresh egg linguine, cooked
⅓ cup ricotta
2 tbsp. fresh basil, chopped
salt and pepper *(if can tolerate)*
2 tbsp. Parmesan cheese

Cook eggplant in olive oil 3-4 min. Add garlic and red pepper. Cook 2-3 minutes. Add ricotta, basil, salt and pepper. Serve over linguine, garnish with Parmesan. Makes 1 serving.

## Fettuccine with Zucchini & Mushrooms (Diane M).

1 lb. pkg. fettuccine
½ c. butter
½ lb. mushrooms
1 ¼ lb. zucchini
1 cup half-and-half
3/4 cup Parmesan cheese, shredded
1/2 cup fresh parsley

Cook fettuccine al dente. Cut zucchini into julienne strips. While pasta is cooking, sauté mushrooms and zucchini in butter for 2 minutes. Add half-and-half to sauté; reduce heat and simmer for 3 minutes. Add cooked fettuccine to sauté, along with cheese and parsley, and toss to mix well.

## Fettuccine Alfredo (Diane M)

12 oz. fettuccine
1 cup evaporated skim milk
½ cup half-and-half

2 tbsp. butter, cut into small pieces
1 ½ cups Parmesan cheese, grated
2 tbsp. snipped fresh chives

Cook the pasta according to the directions on the package. Meanwhile, in a medium saucepan, heat the milk, half-and-half and butter over medium heat just until the butter is melted and the mixture is hot. Gradually stir in 1 ¼ cups of the Parmesan cheese. Cook and stir just until the cheese is melted. Drain the pasta and add the hot pasta to the cheese mixture. Toss until well coated. To serve, transfer the pasta to plates. Sprinkle with the remaining ¼ cup of Parmesan cheese and the chives.

## Linguine with Clam Sauce (Diane M)

8 oz. linguine, cooked and warm
1 tbsp. olive oil
6 large cloves garlic, minced
3 (10-oz.) cans whole baby clams with juices
⅓ cup nonalcoholic white wine *(if can tolerate)*
⅓ cup chicken broth *(IC friendly)*
1 large carrot, shredded
½ tsp. dried oregano
½ cup snipped fresh Italian parsley
salt & pepper *(optional)*

Lightly spray an unheated large skillet with olive oil no-stick spray. Add the oil and heat over medium heat. Add the garlic. Cook and stir for 1 minute. Drain the clams, reserving the juices. Set the clams aside. Add the juices, wine, broth, carrots and oregano to the skillet. Bring to a boil over high heat. Boil about 15 minutes or until the mixture reduces to about 1 ⅓ cups. Stir in the clams and all but 1 tbsp. of the parsley. Simmer about 1 minute or just until heated through. Then stir in the salt and pepper. To serve, transfer the hot pasta to a large bowl. Pour the clam sauce over the pasta and gently toss until well combined. Sprinkle with the remaining 1 tbsp. parsley to garnish.

cream and mix in well. Add the grated Romano cheese and season with salt and pepper as desired. Makes 3-4 servings. This can be made ahead and reheated in a 350°F oven until piping hot.

### Roasted Brussel Sprouts (Nekura)

1 ½ lbs. Brussels sprouts
3 tbsp. good olive oil
1 tbsp. garlic
1 tbsp. rosemary
½ stick of butter, melted
1 tbsp. basil

Preheat oven to 400 degrees F. Cut off the brown ends of the Brussels sprouts and pull off any yellow outer leaves. Mix them in a bowl with the olive oil and other ingredients, melt butter before putting it in. Pour them on a sheet pan and roast for 35 to 40 minutes, until crisp on the outside and tender on the inside. Shake the pan from time to time to brown the sprouts evenly. Add salt or pepper if you can tolerate it.

### Cheesy Red Potato & Dill Au Gratin (bbear)

*I had these ingredients on hand so I gave it a shot and it is sooooo good! It can easily be adjusted to suit your needs.*

6 red potatoes, sliced into ¼ inch slices
4 tbsp unsalted butter
4 tbsp unbleached white flour
2 ½ cups milk
2 cups shredded mild Cheddar cheese
chopped fresh dill

Preheat oven to 400 degrees F (200 degrees C). Butter a 1 quart casserole dish. Layer ½ of the potatoes into bottom of the prepared casserole dish. In a medium size saucepan, melt butter over medium heat. Once butter has fully melted, mix in the flour and stir constantly with a whisk for one minute. Stir in milk. Cook until mixture has thickened (about 7-9 min for me) Do not let boil. Stir in cheese and dill all at once. Continue stirring until melted. Pour cheese sauce over the potatoes, layer rest of potatoes on top and then add the rest of the cheese sauce on top of that. Cover the dish

# Vegetables

### Olive Oil, Garlic & Romano Cheese Mashed Cauliflower (Carole)

1 head cauliflower
4-6 cloves garlic, peeled
⅓ cup extra virgin olive oil
⅓ cup cream
⅓ cup grated Romano (*if can tolerate other wise use Parmesan*) cheese
salt & freshly cracked pepper (*if can tolerate*)

Clean cauliflower and break into large florets pieces. In a large piece of aluminum foil, tightly wrap cauliflower florets and peeled garlic cloves that have been seasoned with salt and pepper and place in 350°F oven. Bake for 45-55 minutes or until tender. Put into casserole dish and mash to desired consistency. Add oil and with aluminum foil. Bake for 70 minutes in preheated oven.

### Easy baked Zucchini (Carole)

Slice the zucchini in half. Slice off the bottom to keep in stable. Brush with olive oil and top with garlic or garlic powder. Top with red pepper slices, salt and pepper to taste and tolerance. Use Mozzarella cheese, Parmesan cheese and sprinkle with basil. Bake 375F for 20 to 30 minutes until soft.

### Sweet Potato Casserole (Carole)

3 cups cooked or canned sweet potatoes mashed
¼ cup brown sugar
½ tsp. salt
1 ½ cup miniature marshmallows
1 tsp. nutmeg (if can tolerate)
1 tsp. cinnamon (if can tolerate)
1/4 cup cream
1 tbsp. butter, melted
1/2 cup pecans, chopped (if can tolerate)

Blend together the sweet potatoes, sugar, salt, spices, butter, cream and half the marshmallows. Spoon into buttered baking dish. Top with pecans and remaining marshmallows. Bake at 350 degrees for about 20 minutes. Marshmallows should be delicately browned.

### Butterscotch Yams (Diane M)

6 medium yams or sweet potatoes (about 3 lbs.), peeled, quartered and cooked or 3 cans (17 oz each) yams, drained
½ cup light or dark corn syrup
½ cup firmly packed brown sugar
¼ cup heavy or whipping cream
2 tbsp. margarine or butter
½ tsp. cinnamon (if can tolerate)

Place yams in 13" x 9" x 2" baking dish. Bake in 325°F oven for 15 minutes.  In small saucepan combine corn syrup, brown sugar, cream, margarine and cinnamon. Stirring constantly, bring to a boil over medium-high heat and boil for 5 minutes. Pour over yams. Bake yams an additional 15 minutes, basting frequently.

### Sesame Carrots and Cabbage (AgilityMe)

*This one turned out really good! Even the kids and hubby like it*

2 medium/large carrots, cut into matchsticks
2 cups shredded green cabbage
1 clove garlic, minced
1 oz. (about 12) raw almonds, roughly chopped
1 tbsp. toasted sesame oil
Salt and pepper to taste (if can tolerate)

Put carrots and garlic in a large pan with just enough water to sauté but not so much that it won't fully evaporate. When carrots begin to soften, add cabbage, almonds and sesame oil. Toss well so the oil coats all the ingredients. Continue to stir/toss until the cabbage softens. Serve and enjoy!

### Squash Dressing (Diane M)

2 cups cornbread crumbled
2 cups squash cooked and mashed
1 small shallot diced (if can tolerate)
¼ tsp. sage
1 can cream of mushroom soup, low sodium
1 can cream of chicken soup, low sodium
1 stick of butter, melted
3 eggs, slightly beaten

Mix all together in a greased pan and bake at 350 degrees for 30 to 40 minutes. If the mixture seems a little dry prior to baking, I add a little bit of low sodium chicken broth or water.

### Broccoli with Garlic & Olive Oil (Diane M)

1 large or 2 small to medium sized broccoli heads
3 tbsp. olive oil
3 garlic cloves, chopped
salt & pepper (if can tolerate)

Trim the broccoli of its tough parts. Peel the stems and cut into bite-size pieces. Break the rest of the broccoli into florets. Steam the broccoli until it is bright green, then remove from the heat and rinse in cold water to cool. Combine the oil and garlic in a saucepan and warm until fragrant, then add the broccoli, salt, and pepper. Stir and cook for 5 minutes or so. Do not let the broccoli cook to a gray color; it should be tender but still green. Serve right away, hot or at room temperature.

## Roasted Garlic (Diane M)

4 large heads of garlic, trimmed to expose the tips of the cloves
¾ cup chicken broth, low sodium
½ tsp. dried thyme
½ tsp. dried rosemary

Place the heads of garlic in a small shallow baking pan. Pour the chicken broth over the garlic, sprinkle with the thyme and rosemary. Cover tightly with foil and bake at 400F (200C) for 1 hour. Cool until they can be safely handled, and squeeze the garlic out of the "paper" husk. Serve hot or cold.

## Spinach with Parmesan and Almonds (Diane M)

1 tbsp. olive oil
2 lbs. washed and trimmed spinach leaves
2 tbsp. grated Parmesan cheese
¼ tsp. salt
¼ tsp. freshly ground black pepper (if can tolerate)
2 tbsp. almonds

Heat the olive oil in a large skillet and add the spinach gradually, turning and stirring until all the leaves are just wilted, about 2 to 3 minutes. Remove from the heat and add the remaining ingredients, tossing to mix well. Serves 4 to 6.

## Roasted Vegetable Calzone (Diane M)

2 tsp. olive oil
1 sweet red pepper, thinly sliced
1 zucchini, thinly sliced
1 yellow summer squash, thinly sliced
1 small onion, thinly sliced (if can tolerate)
2 cloves garlic, minced
salt & pepper (if can tolerate)
1 loaf frozen French bread dough
cornmeal
2 tbsp. crumbled Feta cheese
2 tbsp. shredded part-skim Mozzarella cheese

In a large oven proof frying pan over medium heat, heat the oil and sauté the red peppers, zucchini, squash, onions and garlic for 2 minutes, or until tender. Put the pan in the oven and bake at 500 degrees for 10 minutes, stirring the vegetables occasionally. Remove from the oven. Add salt and black pepper to taste. Allow to cool while shaping the dough. Do not turn off the oven.

Coat a baking sheet with nonstick spray. Place on the lowest rack of the oven. Dust another baking sheet with cornmeal. Divide the French bread dough into 4 pieces. Form into 7-inch rounds. Place the rounds on the cornmeal dusted baking sheet. Spoon the vegetable mixture evenly over half of each round. Sprinkle the Feta and Mozzarella evenly over the vegetable mixture. Brush the outside edges of the rounds with water and fold the dough over the vegetables, pinching the edges to seal. Carefully slide the calzones onto the prepared, preheated baking sheet. Bake for 10 to 12 minutes, or until crisp and brown.

## Stuffed Artichokes (leelee)

medium artichoke
Italian bread crumbs
Parmesan cheese
garlic
olive oil
butter

Cut the tops of the artichokes, turn them upside down and kind of hit them on the counter. This is to open them up to stuff them. This is the only way I know how to explain this! Mix all ingredients together except olive oil and butter. Put the mix in the leaves of the artichoke, fill the leaves pretty full. Place in a baking pan snug with other artichokes. Drizzle olive oil and butter over the artichokes as much as you want to your taste. Add water to pan about half way up, if needed. Cover and bake for about an hour on 350 or until tender. This is the best way to cook them. If they're bigger then cook them longer. You can replace any of the ingredients. It's really good to put minced shrimp or crab meat in them.

## Sweet Potato Fries (Verdicries)

2 pounds sweet potatoes
¼ cup olive oil
2 tsp. coarse sea salt
1 tsp. ground cumin
1/2 tsp. ground mild chili pepper (optional)
sea salt

Set the oven at 500 degrees. Peel the potatoes. Cut them into thick fries, ½" wide by 3 ½" long. In a bowl, combine the potatoes, oil, salt, cumin, and chili powder. Carefully toss to coat them all over. Arrange the potatoes on the baking sheet in a single layer. Bake them, turning so they brown evenly, for 15 to 20 minutes or until the potatoes are crisp and golden. Some also use brown sugar or garlic powder or nutmeg and cinnamon on their fries. I haven't tried that yet. These are YUMMY!!!

## Mushroom Rice Medley (Diane M)

2 cups brown rice
32 oz. (2 cans) chicken broth, low sodium
8 oz. mixed fresh mushrooms (button, shitake, crimini, etc.)
½ cup unsalted pecans or almonds
1 tbsp. olive oil

Heat chicken broth to boiling in a large saucepan. Add rice and cook according to package directions, until tender and all of the broth is absorbed, about 45 minutes. Meanwhile, chop pecans and then set aside. Slice mushrooms into strips. Heat olive oil in a saucepan until hot but not smoking. Add mushrooms and nuts, cook until mushrooms are lightly browned. Combine hot cooked rice with mushroom mixture. Season to taste with salt and pepper and serve immediately.

## Foods High in Vitamin C

Many patients ask how they can obtain enough Vitamin C if they can't eat citrus fruits. That's easy! Focus on the veggies that have high levels of Vitamin C instead. Raw veggies are best but you'll still get good levels after cooking. Here's a list of high C veggies that are, for most patients, also quite bladder friendly!

**Red Bell Peppers (nearly 200mg)**

**Parsley (130mg)**

**Broccoli (90 mg)**

**Green bell peppers (80mg)**

**Brussel Sprouts (80mg)**

**Kale (41mg)**

**Cauliflower (40mg)**

**Raspberries (30mg)**

**Spinach (30mg)**

**Cabbage, raw (30mg)**

**Butternut Squash (21mg)**

**Spaghetti Squash (20mg)**

**Potato (20mg)**

**Zucchini (19mg)**

**Yellow Squash (17mg)**

**Blueberries (10mg)**

**Banana (9mg)**

*(per100mg servings)*

*Source: IC Diet Project*

*www.ic-dietproject.com*

2 tsp. dried parsley
1 tbsp. dried tarragon
salt and pepper to taste
1 small boneless/skinless chicken breast, cubed into 1/2 inch pieces
2 cans of chicken broth (make sure its MSG free/preservative free!)
1 cup of cooked egg noodles

Melt butter in another pan. Sauté onions until almost translucent, then add garlic and sauté for another minute. Add the herbs, carrots and celery and continue to sauté for a couple more minutes. Add the chicken broth and bring to a low simmer. Cook with a lid on for about 20 to 30 minutes until the carrots are tender. Add your peas and green beans and cook for another minute or two. When it's back to a good simmer, throw in your cubed chicken and cook until done (2 to 5 minutes, depending on the size of the chicken pieces. You can always cut one in half to check if it's done. You just don't want to overcook them.) Add your drained noodles. Season with salt and pepper to taste and enjoy!

## White Bean Chicken Chili (Bladderella)

*I made White Bean Chicken Chili over the weekend for the first time. It was absolutely delicious. It doesn't have the heat of traditional chili, but it is very flavorful. My husband raved over it and said he prefers it over my traditional chili. I served it up with a pan of hot, sweet cornbread. I am making a second batch to put in the freezer. Here's the recipe I used:*

3-4 chicken breasts, cooked and chopped into bite-size pieces
3 cans organic pinto beans, drained and rinsed
½ cup chopped sweet onion
3 celery stalks, chopped
1 chopped red pepper
1 32 oz. carton Swanson organic chicken broth
3 minced garlic cloves
1 tbsp. all-purpose flour
1 tsp. cumin
1 tsp. dried oregano
1 tbsp. olive oil
¼ tsp. Hungarian paprika (omit if you can't tolerate)

# Soups

## Simple Chicken Soup (Loveslife)

*Here's a pretty simple recipe that you can vary to your tastes. It does have garlic and onion in it so you need to know your limits. Garlic is usually pretty well tolerated and cooked onion may be tolerated by others including myself. You can always add different veggies or change the seasonings. For me I'd add more garlic but then I love garlic! Try to get a decent MSG free canned chicken broth. If you're feeling really adventurous, you can always cook the broth from scratch with the bones and scraps. Trader Joes has pretty decent chicken broth that comes in cartons too.*

2 tbsp. butter
½ medium onion, diced (if you can tolerate)
3 cloves garlic, minced
1 medium carrot, sliced
1 medium celery stalk, sliced
¼ to ½ cup frozen peas and green beans

¼ tsp. chili powder *(omit if you can't tolerate)*
salt & pepper to taste

In a large pot over medium heat warm the oil. Add chopped veggies and sauté e for 5 min. Add chicken and cook through (at least 5 minutes). Add the garlic, flour, cumin, oregano, paprika, and chili pepper. Cook, stirring over low heat 2 minutes. Add the broth while stirring. Increase heat and bring to a boil stirring occasionally. Reduce heat to simmering and cook 10 minutes longer. Mash one of the cans of beans with a potato masher for thickness. Add the 2 cans of beans and the mashed beans. Season with salt and pepper. Garnish with shredded cheese *(Monterey Jack or mild Cheddar)* and sour cream *(optional)*.

## Honey Carrot Soup (Carole)

1 package (16 oz.) baby carrots, or 3 ½ cups sliced carrots
1 cup chicken stock, low sodium
1 medium onion, chopped *(if can tolerate)*
½ cup milk
¼ cup liquid honey
ground nutmeg to taste *(if can tolerate)*

In a large saucepan, combine carrots, chicken stock and onion. Cover and simmer over medium heat for about 15 minutes or until carrots are tender. Transfer mixture to blender or food processor. Blend until smooth. Return to saucepan. Add milk and honey. Return to simmer. Serve hot or chilled, sprinkled with nutmeg.

## Best Carrot Soup Ever (Briza)

1.5 to 2 lbs. carrots, chopped
4 cups IC safe stock or water
1 medium potato or sweet potato, chopped *(optional, for heartier soup)*
3-4 tbsp. butter, canola or olive oil.
1 cup chopped onion *(use only if tolerated)*
1-2 small cloves crushed garlic *(use only if tolerated)*
⅓ cup pumpkin seed or almonds

Seasoning choices: (use only if tolerated)
2 pinches of nutmeg, 1/2 tsp. dried mint, dash of cinnamon

1 tsp. each of thyme, marjoram and basil
1/2 tsp. dry or 1 tsp. grated ginger
⅓ cup fresh cilantro
1 tsp. orange zest *(use only if tolerated)*

Optional:
1 cup milk, almond milk, coconut milk, half and half, or heavy cream

Place carrots, potato and liquid into a medium sized soup pot and bring to a boil. Cover and simmer until carrots are soft. Let cool to room temperature. Meanwhile, sauté the onion, garlic and nuts in the butter or oil until the onions are clear. Puree everything together in a blender until smooth, or use immersion blender directly in the pot. Return to pot and whisk in seasoning. At this point, you may choose to add milk or cream. However, the soup is so thick and rich with the addition of the nuts. I usually skip this step. Reheat before serving. Garnish with toasted nuts, a splash of cream or spoonful of plain yogurt or sour cream, truffle oil, fresh/dried herbs or spices, some toasted bread crumbs or eat just as it is.

## Bacon Cheddar Cauliflower Chowder (Carole)

8 slices nitrate free bacon, chopped *(half used for garnish)*
½ small onion *(if can tolerate)*
1 celery stalk, chopped
2 garlic cloves, minced
salt & pepper
4 cups shredded or grated cauliflower (½ large head)
2 tbsp. water
2 tbsp. flour
2 cups IC friendly chicken broth, divided
2 cups 2% milk
2 ½ cups shredded Cheddar cheese, divided *(half used for garnish)*

Whisk together flour and ¼ cup chicken broth in a small bowl then set aside. Sauté bacon in a large soup pot over medium heat until crisp. Using a slotted spoon, transfer bacon to a paper towel-lined plate then remove all but 1 tbsp. drippings from the pot. Add chopped onion *(if using)*, celery and garlic to the pot then season with salt and pepper. Sauté until vegetables are tender, about 4-5 minutes.

Add cauliflower and onion powder (if using) to the pot then stir to combine. Add water then place a lid on top and steam cauliflower until tender, stirring a couple times, about 5-7 minutes. Add remaining chicken broth and milk then turn up heat and bring to a boil. Slowly whisk in flour/chicken broth mixture while stirring, then turn down heat and simmer for 3-4 minutes or until chowder has thickened. Turn off heat then stir in 2 cups Cheddar cheese until smooth, then stir in half the cooked bacon. Taste and adjust salt, pepper, and/or hot sauce if necessary. Serve topped with remaining shredded cheese, cooked bacon, and green onions, if desired.

*Use a food processor's chopping and grating blades to make prepping veggies and cheese a breeze*

## Beef Leek Barley Stew (RaiinbowEyes)

*This stuff is incredibly delicious and super filling! I adapted my own recipe from the one on Smitten Kitchen. I've made it many times now, and man oh man is it good! It has a longer cooking time (3 hours) but it's pretty much all just letting the pot simmer while you kick up your feet and relax*

4-8 large meaty short ribs
olive oil
2 onions, chopped
3 cloves of garlic, minced
8 cups beef broth
1 bay leaf
black pepper *(if tolerated)*
½ cup barley
3 russet potatoes, cubed
3 large leeks, washed and chopped *(white and light green parts only)*

Heat olive oil in the bottom of a large pot. Add onion and garlic and sauté for a few minutes, until onions start to turn translucent. Add short ribs and brown on all sides. Add the broth, bay leaf, leeks, and grind in some pepper *(if tolerated)*. Stir, cover and simmer for one hour. Then add half of the potatoes and the barley. Cover for another hour, then add the rest of the potatoes. Simmer one more hour. With the

back of a large spoon or spatula, mush the more well cooked potatoes against the side of the pot to give it a stew like consistency. Remove the short ribs, take the meat off the bones, chop them, and return them to the pot (discard bones). Serve with more ground pepper, if desired.

*I've loved this recipe for a long time and, thankfully, it can be made IC friendly very easily! Just leave the black pepper out if those are a problem for you. If others in your household like spicy things, they can spice it up easily with sriracha and/or black pepper added to their individual bowl. That's what my husband does, he loves his spicy foods! It's easy to make and super yummy, hope you guys enjoy.*

## Fiesta Corn Potato Chowder (Raiinboweyes)

2 cans sweet corn kernels, drained
½ cup diced onion
2 large garlic cloves, minced
3 medium red potatoes, diced into ½" pieces
1 red bell pepper, finely chopped
2 tbsp. olive oil
1 14 oz. can chicken or vegetable broth
1 ½ cup milk
1 tbsp. thyme
1 tbsp. salt
1 tsp. freshly ground black pepper *(if tolerated)*

Heat a large soup pot over medium-high heat and add the oil. When hot, add the onions & garlic and sauté until they become fragrant and just begin to turn translucent. Next, add the potatoes, salt, thyme and black pepper, and cook until the potatoes begin to brown slightly. Add the broth and bring to a low boil. Simmer for about 5 minutes until the potatoes soften. Add the corn kernels and milk and bring back to a low boil.

Remove about ¾ of the soup mixture and carefully puree in a food processor or with a hand (immersion) blender until completely smooth. Return the puree to the pot, add the peppers and bring to a slow simmer for about 5 minutes, stirring occasionally. Remove from heat. Ladle into soup bowls, garnish with freshly ground black pepper. Enjoy!

## Super Easy DIY Vegetable Broth (Tectonic)

I like to steam fresh or frozen vegetables by putting them into a bowl with a little bit of water (¼ cup or less. It depends on the amount of veggies in the bowl) and microwaving them with a loose fitting lid over top until they're heated through. When they're done, there's usually quite a bit of water (and veggie "residue"). Drain that liquid into a plastic container with a lid and pop it into the freezer. It freezes solid, and the next time I steam veggies, I take the container back out and add the fresh veggie-water to it. I repeat the process until I have 4-8 cups in the container. Then I thaw it out and use it as soup stock. It's loaded with nutrients and it's so cheap! It may take awhile before you have enough to make a soup with, but the more veggies you steam, the faster it will fill.

*Experiment with different veggies, and if you can tolerate seasoning, try to customize the flavor.*

## Asian Mushroom Soup (sandberg4)

*This is lowfat, low calorie and good for you too. Plus it tastes wonderful.*

4 cups fat free, reduced sodium chicken broth
3 tbsp. reduced sodium soy sauce
2 tsp. grated fresh ginger
3 garlic cloves, crushed
3 cups assorted mushrooms, sliced (*white buttons, oyster, shitake, portobello and crimini, if using shitake, discard stems.*)
3 cups white cabbage, cut in wedges
1 cup carrots, thinly sliced
2 cups chicken breast, shredded
2 cups fresh udon noodles or cooked linguine
1 cup green onions, thinly sliced
2 cups shredded raw spinach or whole baby spinach leaves
freshly ground black pepper to taste

In a large pot, combine broth, soy sauce, ginger, garlic, mushrooms, cabbage, carrots and chicken. Cover. Bring to a boil. Simmer until mushrooms are soft, about 5 minutes. Stir in noodles, green onions and spinach. Simmer until greens are wilted, about 2 minutes. Season. I make a double pot and freeze it.

## Sweet Potato Pear Soup (Carole)

1 ½ tbsp. butter
2 yellow onions, finely chopped (*if can tolerate*)
2 lbs. sweet potatoes, peeled and diced
4 pears, peeled, cored and diced or 2 (15 oz.) cans pears, without juice
6-8 cups chicken broth, low sodium
1 cup Greek yogurt (*if can tolerate*)
chopped fresh mint or parsley for garnish

Melt the butter in a large pot over a medium heat, and sauté onion for 2-3 minutes until softened. Add the diced sweet potato and diced pear, and sauté for 3-4 minutes. If using canned pears, only sauté the diced sweet potato at this stage and add the pears later. Add the chicken broth to the pot, bring to the boil and simmer gently for 20-25 minutes, or until the sweet potato (and pears) are soft. Cool the soup for about 30 minutes.

If using canned pears, drain these well, reserve the juice and add the pears now. They will help to cool down the soup. In batches, process the chicken broth, sweet potatoes and pears until smooth in a blender or a food processor. Adjust the thickness of the soup so that it is to your liking by adding either more pears or some of the reserved pear juice. Return the soup to the pot. Gently reheat, without boiling, stir in a swirl of yogurt and garnish with fresh mint or parsley.

## Roasted Eggplant Soup (egrolman)

*I made this recipe for roasted eggplant soup today, half inventing it and half using a recipe I found online. All ingredients are IC friendly and the recipe is endlessly variable and very easy to make. I hope you find it useful and as delicious as I found it.*

2 tsp. olive oil
4 cloves garlic
2 stalks of celery and celery leaves
3 carrots, thinly sliced
1 can cannellini or garbanzo beans
1 medium eggplant
chicken or vegetable stock, low sodium

Roast eggplant by cutting it in half and baking it, along with the garlic, on a baking sheet in a 375 degree oven. Drizzle garlic and eggplant with a little olive oil before putting it into the oven. Bake about 25 minutes or until very soft. Scoop out eggplant and mash it with the roasted garlic by hand or by putting it in a blender or Cuisinart. Set aside.

Sauté garlic, carrots, celery and celery leaves for 3-4 minutes. Add 4 cups chicken stock and the can of drained beans. Add the eggplant/garlic mixture. Cook on medium heat until it thickens, stirring occasionally. If you prefer a thinner soup, add water or stock as necessary. Heat until desired serving temperature.

## Split Pea Soup (agilityme)

*This is one of the few IC friendly foods I make that the whole family likes. Well, except for the oldest daughter, but she hates everything. I hope you enjoy it!*

1 tbsp. olive oil
1 onion or leeks, chopped *(optional)*
1 bay leaf
2 cloves garlic, minced
2 cups dried split peas, sorted and rinsed
1-2 cups cooked brown rice
7 ½ cups water
3 carrots, chopped
3 stalks celery, chopped
3 red or gold potatoes, diced
½ cup chopped parsley
½ tsp. dried basil
½ tsp. dried thyme
sea salt & pepper to taste

In a large pot, sauté the onion and garlic in the olive oil until onion is translucent. If you can't have onions, just omit them. Add the water, bay leaf and peas. Bring to a boil then reduce heat and simmer until peas begin to soften. Add the carrots, celery, potatoes, parsley, basil, thyme, sea salt and pepper. Simmer until veggies are tender. Add rice. Serve when thoroughly warm.

## Chicken Tortellini Soup (Diane M)

4 ½ qt. chicken broth, low sodium
1 pkg. (9 oz.) cheese-filled spinach tortellini
¾ lb. stemmed spinach leaves, rinsed well, drained, and chopped
1 lb. boneless and skinless chicken breasts, cut into ½" chunks
½ lb. mushrooms, sliced
1 cup cooked white or brown rice
2 tsp. dry tarragon leaves
grated Parmesan cheese *(if can tolerate)*

In an 8-10 qt. pot, bring chicken broth to a boil over high heat. Add tortellini, cook until al dente. Add spinach, chicken, mushrooms, rice, and tarragon. Return to a boil over high heat. Reduce heat, cover, and simmer until chicken is no longer pink in the center, about 2 minutes. Sprinkle Parmesan cheese, if desired. Serves 10-12.

## Avocado Tortilla Soup (Carole)

1 onion or chives, sliced *(if can tolerate)*
1 cup chicken or beef broth, low sodium
1 cup of water
2 tsp. of butter
½ tsp. of freshly chopped cilantro or parsley leaves
¼ medium avocado, peeled and sliced
8 tortilla chips

Melt the butter in a suitably sized saucepan over medium heat. Separate the onion slices into rings and sauté in the melted butter until they turn a golden color. Add the chicken broth and chopped cilantro leaves. Stir gently to blend. Lower the heat and allow to simmer for 5 minutes. Pour into soup bowls. Add avocado slices and tortilla chips.

## Gypsy Soup and Molasses Bread (Briza)

*Tasty, healthy IC safe meal for cold winter evenings.*

olive oil
1 sweet potato, cut into 1" chunks
½ onion or 4 green onions cut in 1" chunks
1 clove garlic, sliced
2 stalks celery, cut into 1" chunks

4 cups chick or vegetable broth or water
½ can garbanzo beans (drained and rinsed)
1 zucchini sliced lengthwise and then cut in 1"
chunks
½ tsp. turmeric
½ tsp. dried basil
1 bay leaf
½ tsp. cinnamon or pumpkin pie spice

*Leave out onion/garlic if you aren't sure about those.
*Any green and orange veggies will do (carrots & snow peas or
butternut squash & fresh green beans)
*If you don't have turmeric in your pantry no big deal to leave
it out. It adds color but not too much flavor.

Sauté veggies in olive oil for five minutes. Add broth/water, garbanzo beans, zucchini, and spices. Cover and simmer for 10-15 minutes until veggies are done.

Whole wheat molasses bread (makes one bread pan or six Texas sized muffins):
1 ¾ cups whole wheat flour
½ cup all purpose flour
1 tsp. salt
1 ½ tsp. baking soda
1 large egg
¼ cup sugar
⅔ cup molasses
1 ½ cups buttermilk or milk

Preheat oven 375F. Grease pan. Mix the flours, salt, and baking soda in a large bowl. In another bowl, whisk egg, sugar, molasses, and milk until well combined. Add egg mixture to flour mixture and combine until everything is well blended. Pour mixture into greased pan and bake 40-45 minutes for a loaf and 25-30 minutes for large muffins.

## Baked Potato Soup (leelee88)
4 baking potatoes
⅔ cup all-purpose flour
6 cups milk
1 cup Cheddar cheese, divided
1 tsp. salt
½ tsp. black pepper (optional)
1 cup sour or cream cheese
¾ cup chopped green onions, divided
6 bacon slices, cooked and crumbled

Preheat oven to 400F. Pierce potatoes with a fork. Bake for 1 hour or until tender. Cool. Peel potatoes; coarsely mash. Discard skins. Lightly spoon flour into a dry measuring cup; level with a knife. Place flour in a large Dutch oven. Gradually add milk, stirring with a whisk until blended. Cook over medium heat until thick and bubbly (about 8 minutes). Add mashed potatoes, ¾ cup cheese, salt, and pepper, stirring until cheese melts. Remove from heat. Stir in sour cream and ½ cup onions. Cook over low heat 10 minutes or until thoroughly heated (do not boil). Sprinkle each serving with cheese, onions, and bacon.

## Corn and Cheese Chowder (Carole)
5-6 ears corn
2 tbsp. butter
salt/pepper
4 tbsp. salted butter
1 onion, chopped
3 slices IC friendly thick-cut bacon, cut into small pieces
¼ cup flour
4 cups IC friendly chicken broth
⅔ cups half & half
½ cheddar cheese, grated (as tolerated)
chives, sliced for serving time

Preheat oven to 425F for the corn and line a pan with nonstick foil. Melt the 2 tablespoons of butter in the microwave and pour over the corn. Sprinkle generously with salt and pepper and roast for 25-30 minutes, turning occasionally, until browned. Cool a few minutes and then cut the kernels off the cobs.

Melt the butter in a large stockpot. Add the chopped onion and cook a few minutes. On medium-high, add in the bacon and cook until all the bacon pieces are crispy, stirring often. Sprinkle the flour on and stir until it is dissolved. Add the corn and stir well. Put heat on high and add the broth. Let simmer a few minutes. Pour in the half and half. Season with salt and pepper. Cover and lower heat to a simmer for 15 minutes. Remove cover and stir in the cheddar cheese until melted. Serve into bowls and top with chopped chives.

# Salads & Salad Dressings

## SALADS

### Macaroni Salad with Creamy Dressing (Carole)

Add to 4 cups cooked macaroni:
½ cup celery, chopped
½ cup cauliflower, chopped
½ cup red/yellow/orange peppers, chopped
½ cup carrots, chopped
½ to 1 can of albacore (optional)
Set Aside

Creamy Dressing:
In a small saucepan add
1/2 cup whipping cream

2 tsp. cornstarch
¼ tsp. basil
¼ tsp. oregano
¼ tsp. garlic
2 tbsp. cream cheese (in the block form)
1 tbsp. Feta cheese

Heat until thickened. Cool completely. Add the macaroni mixture.

### Kale Salad Recipe (Emilywst)

*I made an IC friendly (strict diet) salad this evening that was actually very good!*

Mix together:
organic baby kale
English cucumbers, thinly sliced
yellow pepper, finely chopped
orange pepper, finely chopped
broccoli, finely chopped
organic blueberries
feta cheese (*not crumbled, but small pieces*)
Dress with olive oil and feta juice.

### Potato Salad with Creamy Dill Dressing (Carole)

3 cups cooked potatoes, chopped
½ cup celery
2 hard boiled eggs, crumbled
½ cup vinegar free pickles, cut into small pieces
(Bubbies or my Bread and Butter pickles)
Set aside

Creamy Dill Dressing:
In a small sauce pan add:
½ cup of whipping cream
2 tsp. cornstarch
2 tsp. of dried dill or 1/2 cup fresh dill
½ tsp. garlic powder
2 tbsp. cream cheese (*in the block*)

Bring to a soft bowl and cook until thickened. Cool completely. Add to potato mixture. Serve and enjoy.

*\*To make Bread and butter pickle cut one large Bubbie's pickle and generously add sugar to coat. Put in sealed container and refrigerate overnight or for several hours. Not everyone can eat Bubbie's pickles or other pickles. If you're not sure you can have*

*them without symptom increase, try the recipe without them! It will still be delicious.*

## Cucumber and Peach Salad (Carole)

*I love peaches! Peaches are on the try it list.*

1 large cucumber, peeled & chopped
2 ripe peaches, chopped(if can tolerate)
1 tbsp. fresh mint, minced
1 tbsp. fresh basil, minced
2 tbsp. pure peach or pear juice *(or 1 tbsp. of each)*

Mix all ingredients in a large bowl and chill in the refrigerator for 30 minutes.

*\* You could also try this salad with my Maple Cream salad dressing, Simply Pear salad dressing or Mock Red Wine salad dressing instead of pear/peach juice.*

## Sweet Pepper Salad (Carole)

*I love the freshness of this salad. It taste so clean. No need for a dressing but if you prefer one you can use one of the dressings I have already posted on this site. The cheese just adds so much flavor. This recipe is serves 1 but you can easily double or triple the recipe.*

Mix:
¼ red pepper, chopped
¼ yellow pepper, chopped
¼ orange pepper, chopped
¼ cup celery, chopped
¼ - ½ cup cucumber, chopped
¼ cup carrots, chopped
¼ - ½ cup Mozzarella cheese, cut into small pieces
Add salt and pepper to taste, mix and serve.

*\* You can add IC friendly cottage cheese, feta or a mixture of all three. Like I always say you can never have enough cheese.*

## Green Bean & Feta Salad (Diane M)

1 lb. fresh green beans
¼ cup green onions(if can tolerate)
½ cup feta cheese
½ cup slivered almonds

Cook beans until tender-crisp, about 5 min. Add onions, cheese and almonds. Drizzle with garlic and basil olive oil. Chill for several hours.

## Pasta Salad with Cucumber Dressing (Carole)

2 skinless, boneless chicken breast halves *(cooked)*
1 (16 oz.) package uncooked farfalle (bow tie) pasta
½ lb. cooked cocktail shrimp
1 (2.25 oz.) can diced black olives, drained
½ cup baby carrots, chopped
1 cucumber, diced
1 (6 oz.) package feta cheese, crumbled
seasoning to taste

Cut chicken into bite size pieces. Bring a large pot of lightly salted water to a boil. Add pasta, cook 8 to 10 minutes, until al dente and drain. Cool to room temperature. In a large bowl, mix the chicken, pasta, shrimp, olives, carrots and cucumber. Toss with feta cheese and season as desired. Serve with Cucumber Dressing

Cucumber Dressing
2 small pickling cucumbers, peeled, seeded, and diced
½ tsp. salt
⅔ cup plain yogurt *(if can tolerate)*
½ tsp. minced fresh mint leaves
½ tsp. minced fresh dill

Place the cucumber in a colander, sprinkle with salt and allow to drain for 15 minutes. Mix the yogurt, mint, and dill in a bowl. Stir in the drained cucumber. Chill at least 30 minutes before serving. This dressing is also good for putting in wraps or as a salad dressing.

*\*if you can't tolerate the yogurt you can try sour cream or kefir if you can tolerate those.*

# SALAD DRESSINGS

## Hummus Salad Dressing (Briza)

¼ cup extra virgin olive oil
½ can garbanzo beans *(drained and rinsed)*
⅓ cup + 1 tbsp. water
2 tbsp. tahini *(sesame seed paste)* or natural almond butter *(preferably one that does not contain sugar or other ingredients besides salt)*
1-2 cloves garlic

1 tsp. paprika (optional)
¼ cup fresh chopped parsley or kale, or 1 tbsp. dry parsley

Throw everything except parsley in a blender and puree until smooth. Adjust liquids or add more beans to make it to your desired thickness. Stir in parsley by hand. Drizzle it on salads, avocado, or whatever, and garnish with paprika.

## Chip Dip or Salad Dressing (Jenn)

*Ok so I have came up with this dressing/chip dip that I absolutely love and I have to share! I use this on chicken salads, plain potato chips, even crackers. Some ingredients may not be bladder friendly for all but I have found the stuff I put in this doesn't bother me. Feel free to adjust or change up to suit you better!*

1 pkg of fat free cream cheese
1 4 oz. container of feta cheese
½ cup of milk
½ tsp. garlic powder *(if can tolerate)*
¾ tps. onion powder *(if can tolerate)*
1-2 tsp. freeze dried chives
½ tsp. parsley

Put all in a food processor and blend very well. I use a little more milk adding a little at time when making dressing to make it a little runnier. You can adjust herbs to your personal taste.

## Cheesy Dill Salad Dressing (Carole)

2 tbsp. cream
1 tsp. butter
½ tsp. dried dill
1 tbsp. cream cheese

In a microwave safe bowl combine the above ingredients and heat for 30 seconds. Mix well. Cool and serve.

## Cottage Cheese Salad Dressing (Diane M.)

1 cup cottage cheese
1 to 2 tbsp. olive oil
fresh herbs to taste *(I use fresh basil and dried dill weed)*

Salt *(optional)*

Pour into blender. Blend until smooth. Serve with finely shredded lettuce.

## Roasted Garlic Olive Oil Dressing (Diane M)

Use one garlic bulb for each cup of olive oil. After cutting off the top of the bulb, wrap the bulb in foil after drizzling it with olive oil. Bake at 400 for 45 minutes to 1 hour. Once cooled, squeeze the garlic into a container and add the oil. I use a catsup style squeeze bottle. Keep refrigerated. Should be ready to use after a day or two.

## Root Beer Cream Salad Dressing (Carole)

2 tbsp. coconut milk
1 tbsp. root beer
1 tbsp. marshmallow fluff
½ tsp. cornstarch

In a microwave safe bowl add the first 3 ingredients together. Heat for 30 seconds. Add cornstarch and heat another 30 seconds. Cool and Serve.

## Cheese Lovers Salad Dressing (Carole)

2 tbsp. cream
1 tbsp. cream cheese
½ tbsp. feta cheese
1 tsp. Parmesan cheese

Mix all ingredients together and heat in a microwave safe bowl for 30 seconds. Cool and serve.

## Creamy Dilly Cucumber Dressing (Carole)

Cucumber
Cut about a one inch chunk of peeled cucumber into thin slices. Sprinkle lightly with salt and let sit in a bowl for about 20 minutes. Rinse extremely well under water (or your dressing will be salty).

In a blender:
3 tbsp. cream
1/4 tsp. dill
rinsed off cucumbers.

Blend well in a food processor. Transfer to a microwave safe bowl and add ½ cornstarch. Heat for 30 seconds. Cool and serve.

## Mock Red Wine Salad Dressing (Carole)

2 tbsp. olive oil
1 tbsp. blueberry juice
½ tsp. white sugar

Mix well and serve.

## Tropical Cream Salad Dressing (Carole)

½ tbsp. blueberry juice
½ tbsp. pear juice
½ tbsp. honey
1 tbsp. marshmallow fluff
2 tbsp. cream
¾ tsp. cornstarch
1 tbsp. coconut oil

Mix first 5 ingredients in microwave safe bowl and heat for 30 seconds. Add cornstarch and heat another 20 seconds. Mix in coconut oil. Cool and serve.

## Cheesy Garlic Salad Dressing (Carole)

2 tbsp. cream
¼ tsp. garlic powder
1 tsp. butter
½ tbsp. Feta cheese
½ tbsp. cream cheese
¼ tsp. cornstarch

In a microwave safe bowl, mix the first 5 ingredients together and heat for 30 seconds. Add cornstarch and heat another 30 seconds. Cool and serve.

century. English muffin bread has a coarser texture than regular bread and is delicious! The best part is that it makes great toast. The coarseness of the bread, when toasted, provides the perfect backdrop for butter, marmalade, jam or whatever you want to put on it." I read that and my mouth started watering!!

5 ½ cups warm water
3 packages rapid rise yeast
2 tbsp. salt
3 tbsp. sugar
11 cups flour (You can use bread or all-purpose flour. If you substitute wheat flour, use ⅔ bread flour and ⅓ wheat bread flour)

Mix ingredients all together, only enough to combine. Dough will be very sticky. Spoon into 4 regular-sized, well-greased loaf pans or 8 mini-loaf pans. Let rise in pans until dough reaches the top of the pans. Bake in 350F oven for 45 minutes or until golden brown. 10 minutes before done, brush with melted butter. Bread will be moist at first. Cool completely before cutting.

*You can use regular yeast, but you will need to let is rise twice: once in the bowl, till it reaches the top and then again in the pans, till it reaches the top. With the rapid rise yeast, you only need to let it rise once in the pans. Water should be between 120-130 degrees.

## Sausage Asiago Bubble Bread (Carole)

24 frozen IC friendly dinner rolls, thawed but still cold
1 lb. IC friendly nitrate free sausage
¼ cup sweet onion, minced (if can tolerate)
½ cup grated Parmesan cheese (if can tolerate)
1 tsp. dry Italian seasoning (if can tolerate otherwise just use what you can tolerate)
1 tsp. garlic powder
½ tsp. onion powder (if can tolerate)
½ tsp. garlic
2 cups shredded Mozzerella cheese, divided
1 cup finely shredded Asiago cheese, divided (if can tolerate otherwise use a cheese of your choice)
½ cup butter, melted

Arrange the frozen rolls on a sheet of wax paper on the counter. Thaw for 20-30 minutes,

# Breads, Muffins & Scones

## BREAD

### My Mom's Wonderful English Muffin Bread (Bladderella)

I have been craving English muffins but no matter what brand I want to buy, they are all made with ingredients toxic to my IC bladder (i.e., vinegar, soy flour, thiamin mononitrate, calcium propionate, and sorbic acid). I've tried to eat them and have suffered. So imagine my delight when I stumbled across some recipes for English Muffin bread!! One recipe describes the bread like this: "English Muffin Bread is basically an English Muffin in bread form. English muffins have been around for a while and date back to the 10th then use a sharp knife and quarter. In a large skillet, cook the sausage and minced onion until no pink remains. Drain all excess fat from the pan. Set aside to cool, or this can be done in advance and chilled, if preferred. Into a gallon size plastic storage bag, shake together the grated Parmesan cheese, dry Italian seasoning, garlic powder, onion powder and garlic salt. Toss the bread pieces in the melted butter then add to the cheese mixture. Seal and shake until coated.

Spriz the bottom and sides of a non-stick 9" x 13" metal baking pan with cooking spray. Arrange ½ of the quartered rolls on the bottom of the pan. At this point, they won't touch, the bread still has to rise. Over the rolls, sprinkle ⅓ of the shredded mozzarella cheese, ½ of the Asiago cheese and ½ of the crumbled sausage. Repeat, ending with the final ⅓ of shredded Mozzarella cheese and Asiago.

Cover with plastic wrap and allow the rolls to rise in a draft free place until doubled. Around 1 ½ - 2 hours. Uncover and bake at 375F for 35-40 minutes or until puffy and golden. Pull apart and serve. Can dip in basic Nomato sauce recipe.

## Pear Bread (Carole)

3 cups all-purpose flour
1 tsp. baking soda
¼ tsp. baking powder
1 tsp. salt
1 tbsp. cinnamon (if can tolerate)
¾ cup vegetable oil
3 eggs, slightly beaten
2 cups sugar
2 cups pears, peeled and grated
1 cup nuts, chopped
2 tsp. vanilla

Combine flour, soda, baking powder, salt and cinnamon in a large bowl. Make a well in the center of mixture. Combine oil, eggs, sugar, pears, nuts and vanilla. Add to dry ingredients, stirring just until moistened. Spoon mixture into 2 greased 8½" x 4½" x 3" loaf pans. Bake at 325F for 1 hour and 10 minutes or until done.

Cool 10 minutes before removing from pans. Yields: 2 loaves.

## Old Fashioned Potato Bread (Carole)

3 medium white potatoes, peeled and cubed
2 cups warm (110F) water or potato water
2 tbsp. shortening
2 ¼ tsp. or 1 pkg. (¼ oz.) active dry yeast
2 tbsp. sugar
1 tbsp. salt
6 ½ cups bread flour
egg white, lightly beaten

Put cubed potatoes in large saucepan with 2 ½ cups of water. Bring to boil and reduce heat to a simmer for 15 minutes or until potatoes break apart when stuck with a fork. Drain potatoes, reserving 2 cups of the potato water. Mash potatoes with a fork and put in large bowl. Add potato water to bowl. If there is not enough potato water to make 2 cups, add more water to make 2 cups. Add shortening to bowl and stir until dissolved. Set bowl aside until the potato mix is lukewarm or 110F.

Stir in yeast, sugar, and salt. Mix in enough bread flour to make a thick dough that can be kneaded by hand. Turn dough out onto board and knead for 8 minutes, breaking up any large clumps of potato with your fingers. Put dough in greased bowl and turn dough over in the bowl so that the dough top is also lightly greased. Cover with clean kitchen towel and let rise for 1 hour in a warm, draft-free place.

Punch down. Turn dough out onto lightly floured board and knead out bubbles for 5 minutes. Divide dough in half. Form each half into a loaf. Set each loaf into a greased 5 ¼" x 9" x 2 ¾" loaf pan. Cover loaves with kitchen towel and let rise in a warm, draft-free place for 30-45 minutes or until dough is double in bulk.

Uncover bread and brush on egg white for glossy look. Bake at 375F for 45 minutes or until bread sounds hollow when tapped on. Let bread cool on rack. Serve warm or cold.

## Pear Cardamom Bread (Kelly B)

1 ⅔ cups Gold Medal All-Purpose Flour

¾ cup sugar
1 ½ tsp. baking powder
¾ tsp. salt
1 tsp. ground cardamom
1 ½ cups chopped unpeeled pear (1 large)
½ cup vegetable oil
¼ cup milk
2 eggs
Cardamom Topping (below)

Heat oven to 350F. Grease bottom only of loaf pan with shortening. Mix all ingredients except Cardamom Topping in large bowl; beat 30 seconds with spoon. Pour into pan. Make Cardamom Topping; sprinkle over top. Bake 8-inch loaf 50-55 minutes; 9-inch 60-65, or until toothpick inserted in center comes out clean. Cool 10 minutes. Remove from pan to wire rack. Cool loaf completely about 1 hour.

Cardamom Topping:
1 tbsp. sugar
1/4 tsp. ground cardamom
Mix sugar and cardamom in small bowl.

## Homemade Cinnamon Bread (Carole)

1 cup milk
6 tbsp. butter
2 ½ tsp. active dry yeast
2 whole eggs
⅓ cup sugar
3 ½ cups all-purpose flour
1 tsp. salt
⅓ cup sugar
2 tbsp. cinnamon (if can tolerate)
egg and milk, mixed together, for brushing
softened butter, for smearing and greasing

Melt butter with milk. Heat until very warm, but don't boil. Allow to cool until still warm to the touch, but not hot. Sprinkle yeast over the top, stir gently, and allow to sit for 10 minutes. Combine flour and salt. In the bowl of an electric mixer, mix sugar and eggs with the paddle attachment until combined. Pour in milk, butter and yeast mixture and stir to combine. Add half the flour and beat on medium speed until combined. Add the other half and beat until combined. Switch to the dough hook attachment and knead dough on

medium speed for ten minutes. If dough is overly sticky, add ¼ cup flour and beat again for 5 minutes.

Heat a metal or glass mixing bowl so it's warm. Drizzle in a little canola oil, then toss the dough in the oil to coat. Cover bowl in plastic wrap and set it in a warm, hospitable place for at least 2 hours. Turn dough out onto the work surface. Roll into a neat rectangle no wider than the loaf pan you're going to use, and about 18 to 24 inches long. Smear with 2 tbsp. melted butter. Mix sugar and cinnamon together, then sprinkle evenly over the butter-smeared dough. Starting at the far end, roll dough toward you, keeping it tight and contained. Pinch seam to seal. Smear loaf pan with softened butter. Place dough, seam down, in the pan. Cover with plastic wrap and allow to rise for 2 hours.

Preheat oven to 350F. Mix a little egg with milk, and smear over the top. Bake for 40 minutes on a middle/lower rack in the oven. Remove from the pan and allow bread to cool. Slice and serve, or make cinnamon toast or French toast with it.

## Apple Cinnamon Bread (Carole)

⅓ cup brown sugar (not packed)
1 tsp. ground cinnamon (if can tolerate)
⅔ cup white sugar
½ cup butter, softened
2 eggs
1 ½ tsp. vanilla extract
1 ½ cups all-purpose flour
1 ¾ tsp. baking powder
½ cup milk
1 apple, peeled and chopped (Use the lower acid Gala or Fuji apples)

Preheat oven to 350F. Grease and flour a 9" x 5" loaf pan. Mix brown sugar and cinnamon together in a bowl and set aside. Beat white sugar and butter together in a bowl using an electric mixer until smooth and creamy. Beat in eggs, one at a time, until incorporated. Add vanilla extract. Combine flour and baking powder together in another bowl. Stir into creamed butter mixture. Mix milk into batter until smooth. Pour half the batter into the prepared loaf pan. Add half the apples and half the brown sugar cinnamon mixture. Lightly pat apple mixture into batter. Pour the remaining batter over apple layer; top with remaining apples and add more brown sugar/cinnamon mixture. Lightly pat apples into batter. Swirl brown sugar mixture through apples using a finger or spoon. Bake in the preheated oven until a toothpick inserted in the center of the loaf comes out clean, 30 to 40 minutes.

## Pumpkin Bread (Verdicries)

1 ½ cups flour
½ tsp. of salt
1 cup sugar
1 tsp. baking soda
1 cup pumpkin puree
½ cup olive oil
2 eggs, beaten
¼ cup water
½ tsp. nutmeg (it's on the "may be okay" column; I seem to tolerate it)
½ tsp. cinnamon
½ tsp. allspice
½ cup chopped walnuts (I eliminate these)

Preheat oven to 350F. Sift together the flour, salt, sugar, and baking soda. Mix the pumpkin, oil, eggs, ¼ cup of water, and spices together, then combine with the dry ingredients. Stir in the nuts, unless you decide to leave them out! Pour into a well-buttered 9" x 5" x 3" inch loaf pan. Bake 50-60 minutes until a toothpick comes out clean. Let cool on a rack. Makes one loaf.

## Focaccia Bread (Diane M)

¼ cup olive oil
1 onion chopped
½ tsp. granulated sugar
1 ½ cups warm water
1 ½ tsp. active dry yeast
2 tbsp. olive oil
½ tsp. salt
3 cups all-purpose flour
1 tbsp. chopped fresh rosemary
cornmeal
coarse salt

In skillet, heat ¼ cup olive oil over low heat. Cook onion, stirring occasionally, for about 30 minutes or until golden. Let cool. Meanwhile, in large bowl, dissolve sugar in warm water. Sprinkle with yeast and let stand for 10 minutes or until frothy. Stir in 2 tbsp. olive oil and salt. Add 2 cups of the flour and beat with electric mixer for 2 minutes or until smooth and elastic. Gradually stir in remaining flour, onions and rosemary. Turn out onto lightly floured surface and knead lightly until smooth and elastic, adding flour as needed for 8 to 10 minutes. Place in greased bowl, turning to grease all over. Cover and let rise for 35 to 45 minutes. Punch down. Divide in half. Pat each half into flat round. Let rest for 5 minute. Stretch into 10-inch rounds. Place on greased baking sheets sprinkled with cornmeal. Cover and let rise for 35 to 45 minutes. Brush tops with olive oil. Sprinkle with coarse salt and rosemary. Bake in 375F (190C) oven for 25 to 30 minutes or until bottom is browned and crisp. Let stand for 10 minutes. Cut into wedges to serve. Makes 2 rounds.

## Irish Soda Bread (Diane M)

2 ½ cups whole wheat flour
1 cup all-purpose flour
2 tbsp. sugar
1 ½ tsp. baking soda
1 tsp. salt
4 tbsp. butter (room temperature)
1 egg
1 ¼ cups buttermilk (room temperature, if can tolerate)

Mix together all the dry ingredients in a large bowl. Using your fingertips, work the butter into the flour mixture until the mixture resembles breadcrumbs. Beat the egg and buttermilk in a separate bowl, and gradually add to the flour mixture. Mix with a spoon at first, and then by hand or mixer when the dough becomes stiff. On a lightly floured work surface, work the dough to thoroughly blend all the ingredients. Do not knead. Sprinkle with flour if the dough should stick. Shape into a round ball and pat the top down slightly, and place on a greased or baking sheet. Cut a ½" (1 cm) deep cross in the top using a sharp knife or razor blade. Bake in 400F (200C) oven for about 45 minutes, or until it has browned and the cuts have expanded. Remove from oven and cool on a wire rack before slicing.

## Heavenly Coconut Date Bread (Loveslife)

¼ cup soft butter
1 cup pitted dates, chopped
¼ cup brown sugar
¼ cup granulated sugar
¾ cup boiling water
1 egg, beaten
2 cups flour
2 tsp. baking powder
½ tsp. salt
½ cup chopped walnuts (optional)
1 cup unsulphured coconut
1 tbsp. plus 1 tsp. vanilla

Preheat oven to 350F. Put butter, dates and sugars in a bowl. Pour the hot water over them, stirring to cover them. Let them sit for 7 minutes. When cool, add the egg and mix well. Add the flour, baking powder and salt and stir just to incorporate. Add vanilla, nuts and coconut. Stir to mix in. Pour into a buttered loaf pan.

Bake at 350F for 45 to 50 min or until a toothpick comes clean when stuck in the center. Let it cool slightly before you remove it from the pan. Try not to eat it all at once!

# MUFFINS, BISCUITS & SCONES

## Blueberry Cornbread Muffins (Carole)

1 cup yellow corn meal
½ cup all-purpose flour
1 tsp. salt
1 tbsp. baking powder
2 tbsp. sugar
1 cup buttermilk (if can tolerate)
½ cup milk
½ tsp. baking soda
1 whole egg
¼ cup shortening, melted
½ tsp. vanilla
8 oz. dried blueberries (make sure nitrate free)

Vanilla Butter
1 stick ½ cup butter, softened
1 whole vanilla bean
2 tbsp. sugar

Preheat oven to 400F. Combine corn meal, flour, salt, and baking powder in a mixing bowl. In a separate bowl, combine buttermilk, milk, egg, and baking soda. Stir to combine. Add melted shortening, stirring constantly. Add vanilla extract, then stir in dried blueberries. You can use a little more or a little fewer if you'd like. Pour into a greased mini-muffin pan, trying to make sure blueberries stay evenly distributed. Bake for 10 minutes or until golden brown.

To make the vanilla butter, combine the softened butter, the caviar from the vanilla bean, and the sugar. Stir until totally combined, then spread into a ramekin and serve with the vanilla butter.

## Oatmeal Muffins (icnmgrjill)

Combine in small bowl:
1 egg
¾ cup milk
¼ cup Canola oil

Combine in large bowl:
1 cup preservative free flour (Arrowhead Mill® brand)
½ tsp. baking soda
1 tsp. baking powder
½ tsp. salt
⅓ cup brown sugar
1 cup rolled oatmeal

Add egg mixture to dry and stir until moistened. Put in greased tins or use baking cups for easy clean up. Bake at 400F for 15-20 minutes. Yield 12 muffins.

You may also vary this recipe by adding:
1 ½ grated pears
½ tsp. cinnamon

### Cottage Cheese Biscuits (Carole)

*Found this recipe. I love biscuits. I made minor changes to make it IC friendly.*

2 cups all purpose flour
½ tsp. coarse salt
1 tbsp. baking powder
5 tbsp. unsalted butter, cold, cut into small pieces
1 16-oz. container cottage cheese *(make sure IC friendly)*

Preheat oven to 450F. In a large bowl or the bowl place flour, salt and baking powder. Stir until combined. Add butter and mix until it's the size of small peas. Add the cottage cheese and stir until just combined. Using a large soup spoon, drop onto a non-stick cookie sheet. Bake until golden, about 12-15 minutes. Serve immediately.

*\*Variation: could add tolerated herbs of your choice.*

### Red Lobster Cheddar Bay Biscuits (Carole)

2 ½ cups Bisquick® baking mix
4 tbsp. cold butter
1 cup sharp Cheddar cheese, grated *(if can tolerate otherwise use mild)*
¾ cup cold whole milk
¼ tsp. garlic powder

Brush on top:
2 tbsp. butter, melted
½ tsp. garlic powder
¼ tsp. dried parsley flakes
1 pinch salt

Preheat oven to 400F.  Combine Bisquick and cold butter. Don't combine too thoroughly. There should be small chunks of butter about the size of peas. Add Cheddar, milk and ¼ tsp. garlic. Mix by hand until combined, but don't over mix. Drop 9 equal portions onto greased cookie sheet. Bake for 15-17 minutes or until tops are light brown. Melt 2 tbsp. butter in a bowl. Stir in ½ tsp. garlic powder and parsley flakes. Use a pastry brush to spread garlic butter over tops of biscuits.

### Bacon Cheese Biscuit (Carole)

*Found this recipe I made minor changes to make it IC friendly!*

4 slices thick-cut bacon, nitrate free
2 cups all-purpose flour, plus more for dusting
2 tsp. baking powder
¼ tsp. baking soda
1 tsp. kosher salt
1 tbsp. chopped fresh chives
6 tbsp. cold unsalted butter, cut into small pieces, plus melted butter for brushing
1 cup grated Cheddar cheese
1 cup buttermilk *(if can tolerate)*

Preheat the oven to 425F. Cook the bacon in a skillet over medium heat until crisp. Drain on paper towels and reserve 2 tbsp. drippings. Finely chop the bacon. Whisk the flour, baking powder, baking soda, salt, chopped bacon and chives in a medium bowl. Using a pastry blender or your fingers, work the butter into the flour mixture until it is in pea-size pieces. Stir in the cheese with a wooden spoon. Add the buttermilk and reserved bacon drippings and gently mix until just moistened. The dough will be loose.

Turn the dough out onto a lightly floured surface and knead 3 to 5 times, just until it comes together. (Don't over knead or the biscuits will be tough.) Roll out to ½" thick, then cut out biscuits using a floured 2" round cutter. Arrange on an ungreased baking sheet. Re-roll the scraps and cut out more biscuits. Brush the tops with melted butter. Bake the biscuits until golden brown, 12 to 15 minutes. Serve warm.

### Blueberry Scones (Hazel)

I just experimented and made some sugar free blueberry, apple and pear scones and they were surprisingly yummy with a dob if margarine. All I did was cook an assortment of fresh blueberries, apple and pear chunks in the microwave until soft. I combined 1 ½ cups of flour with 2 tbsp. margarine and enough spoonfuls of the blended fruit until the mix was kneadable. Rolled the dough out flat, cut into scone shapes. Brushed the top with milk and cooked at 350 for ten minutes.

## Cheddar Cheese Scones (Carole)

*I made these the other day and I loved them. SOOOOOO GOOOOOD! Easy to make!*

2 cups flour
¼ cup sugar
4 tsp. baking powder
½ tsp. salt
1 tsp. garlic powder (*other spices as desired I also use Basil, Oregano*)
¼ cup cold butter
1 cup, plus ¼ cup grated Cheddar cheese (*or use Mozzarella if can't tolerate Cheddar*)
1 egg, beaten until frothy
⅔ cup milk

In a large bowl mix flour, sugar, baking powder, salt and garlic powder. Add butter and cut in until crumbly using two knives or your hands. Add grated cheese and stir until well mixed. Make a well in centre. Pour egg and milk into well. Using a fork stir in flour gradually to make a soft dough. Turn out on a lightly floured surface and knead 8 to 10 times. Divide into 2 equal parts and pat each into 6" circle. Transfer to a greased baking sheet and brush tops with milk. Sprinkle with ¼ cup grated cheese. Bake in a preheated 425F oven for 15 min.

Cardamom Topping:
1 tbsp. sugar
1/4 tsp. ground cardamom
Mix sugar and cardamom in small bowl.

## Apple Scones (Carole)

2 cups flour
½ cup + 1 tsp. granulated sugar
1 ½ tsp. baking powder
¾ tsp. ground cinnamon (*if can tolerate*)
½ tsp. salt
2 tbsp. cold butter cut into small pieces
⅔ cup half and half cream
¼ cup IC friendly applesauce
1 Gala apple cored and chopped (1 ½ cups)
⅔ cup confectioners sugar

Preheat over to 400F. Grease baking sheet. In bowl, combine flour, ½ cup granulated sugar, baking powder, cinnamon and salt. On medium speed, beat in butter until mixture resembles coarse meal. Beat in cream and applesauce until blended (2 minutes). Stir in apple. Drop batter by ¼ cup fulls onto baking sheet 2 inches apart. Sprinkle top with remaining 1 tsp. granulated sugar. Bake 10-12 minutes until golden brown. Cool. Combine confectioners sugar and 1 tbsp. water, drizzle over scones.

# Dessert

## CAKES & CUPCAKES

### Oatmeal Cake (Robin)

*This is a really old recipe from my mom and I just realized this is one recipe that I can adapt to be IC friendly. It is really good and moist.*

1 cup old fashioned oatmeal
1 stick of oleo/butter
1 ¼ cup boiling water
Mix and let stand for 20 minutes

<u>Cream together</u>
1 cup sugar
1 cup brown sugar
2 eggs
1 tsp. vanilla

<u>Mix together and then add to above:</u>
1 ⅓ cup flour
1 tsp. soda
1 tsp. cinnamon
½ tsp. nutmeg *(if tolerated)*
1 tsp. baking powder
½ tsp. salt

Pour into 9" x 13" pan and bake at 350F for 25-30 minutes.

<u>Topping</u>
6 tbsp. butter/oleo
½ cup sugar
¼ cup hot milk
½ tsp. vanilla
½ cup coconut *(with no preservatives)*

When you take it out of the oven, pour topping over baked cake. Broil for a few minutes until brown. Be sure and watch this because it will burn real easily.

### Applesauce Cake (Diane M)

½ cup vegetable oil *(I used canola)*
¾ cup sugar
1 ½ cup applesauce *(if can tolerate)*
1 ½ tsp. baking soda
¼ tsp. salt
1 tsp. vanilla
2 cups flour
½ tsp. baking powder
½ tsp. cinnamon *(if can tolerate)*
1 cup chopped nuts and raisins *(if can tolerate)*

Mix well all ingredients except nuts and raisins in a large bowl. Fold in nuts and raisins. Bake in 8" x 8" pan for 30-40 minutes at 350 degrees.

### Fluffy Yellow Cupcakes (Bladderella)

*I made these over Christmas and my family loved them. Makes 24-30 cupcakes*

1 cup unsalted butter, softened
2 cups white sugar
2 eggs, separated and at room temperature
3 tsp. pure vanilla extract
2 cups sifted cake flour *(Swans Down)*

1 tbsp. baking powder
1 tsp. salt
1 cup buttermilk, room temperature

*I used SACO Cultured Buttermilk blend. It comes in powder form and is found in spices/baking aisle. To make 1 cup buttermilk, follow instructions on the container (4 tbsp. of SACO and 1 cup water).*

Preheat oven to 325F. Line two cupcake pans with paper cupcake liners.  In a large bowl, cream together butter and sugar. Add in egg yolks and vanilla, mixing until fully incorporated. Set aside. In a separate bowl combine flour, baking powder, salt and buttermilk blend. Gradually add dry ingredients into wet ingredients, alternating with the water. Mix until batter is fluffy but be careful not to over mix. Beat egg whites until foamy and thick. Very gently fold egg whites into batter and mix JUST until incorporated.

Pour batter into cupcake pans, filling each cupcake holder halfway full. Bake for 30-35 minutes. Remove from oven and let cupcakes cool in pans until pans are cool to the touch. When cupcakes are completely cooled, remove them from the pan and frost with buttercream frosting.

Classic Vanilla Buttercream Frosting
1 cup unsalted butter, softened but not melted
3-4 cups confectioners (powdered) sugar, sifted
¼ tsp. table salt
1 tbsp. vanilla extract
up to 4 tbsp. milk or heavy cream

Beat butter for a few minutes with a mixer on medium speed. Add 3 cups of powdered sugar and turn your mixer on the lowest speed until the sugar has been incorporated with the butter. Increase mixer speed to medium and add vanilla extract, salt, and 2 tbsp. of milk/cream and beat for 3 minutes. If your frosting needs a more stiff consistency, add remaining sugar. If your frosting needs to be thinned out, add remaining milk 1 tbsp. at a time.

Banana Cupcakes with Peanut Butter Frosting (Carole)
1 cup granulated sugar
½ cup unsalted butter, softened
2 eggs
½ tsp. vanilla extract
¼ cup kefir, plain yogurt or buttermilk (*if can tolerate*)
2 ripe bananas, cut into small pieces
1 and ½ cups all-purpose flour
1 tsp. baking soda
¾ tsp. cinnamon (*if can tolerate*)
¼ tsp. nutmeg
¼ tsp. salt

Frosting
10 oz. soft cream cheese
1 stick soft unsalted butter
5 cups powdered sugar/confectioners sugar
⅔ cup creamy peanut butter

Preheat your oven to 350F and prepare a muffin tin by lining it with paper liners. With your mixer, cream together butter and sugar until light and fluffy. Add in eggs one at a time, and vanilla and mix to combine. Add in kefir, yogurt or buttermilk and bananas and mix again, making sure to scrape down the sides of the bowl to ensure everything is getting mixed well.

In a large bowl sift together flour, baking soda, cinnamon, nutmeg and salt. Slowly add the dry ingredients to the wet and mix until smooth. Fill each muffin cup about ¾ of the way full. You should get about 15 cupcakes from one batch. Bake for about 18-20 minutes or until a toothpick inserted into the center of the cupcakes comes out clean. Allow the cupcakes to cool for a few minutes before transferring them to a wire rack to cool completely. While the cupcakes cool, make the frosting.

Frosting
With your mixer, combine cream cheese and butter until light and fluffy. Add in powdered sugar, one cup at a time. When all of the powdered sugar has been added and the

71

frosting is light and fluffy, add in ⅔ cup creamy peanut butter and mix to combine.

## Pecan Pie cupcakes (Carole)

1 cup chopped pecans (*if can tolerate*)
½ cup all-purpose flour
1 cup packed brown sugar
⅔ cup butter, melted
2 eggs

Preheat oven to 350F. In a medium bowl, combine all ingredients and mix well. Spray a miniature muffin tin with non-stick cooking spray. The spray with flour in it works best! Fill each ¾ full. Bake in preheated oven for approximately 18 minutes. Once they come out of the oven let them cool for one minute then flip them out onto a cooling rack. If they cool in the pan they'll have to be chiseled out. Also don't fill the pan to the very top. They will overflow if you do.

## Peach Cupcakes with Peach Buttercream Frosting (Carole)

1 ½ cups cake flour
¾ tsp. baking powder
¾ tsp. baking soda
½ tsp. salt
pinch of nutmeg (*if can tolerate*)
pinch of cinnamon (*if can tolerate*)
6 tbsp. butter, room temp.
¼ + 1/8 cups sugar
¼ + 1/8 cups lightly packed brown sugar
1 large eaten, beaten
½ tsp. vanilla extract (*I always add a little more than it says*)
¾ sour cream (*if can tolerate*)
2 medium peaches, peeled, cored, and chopped

Preheat oven to 350F. Line tins with paper liners and set aside. Mix together flour, baking powder, baking soda, salt, nutmeg and cinnamon. Cream together butter and sugar, beating until fluffy. Add the egg, scraping down the sides of the bowl. Next add the vanilla, and slowly mix in the sour cream. Stir in dry ingredients and gently fold in the peaches. Divide the batter evenly among cupcake tins,

about ⅔ full. Bake for 18-22 minutes or until toothpick comes out clean.

## Peach Buttercream

¾ cup butter, at room temperature
1 ½ cups confectioner's sugar
¼ cup peach puree (1-2 peaches)
vanilla extract (to taste)

Beat butter until light and fluffy. Add the sugar and beat until well combined. Add peach puree and vanilla and mix until smooth.

## Blueberry Crumb Cake (Carole)

1/2 stick Butter
1 tbsp. (additional) Butter
3/4 cups Sugar
1 whole Egg
1/2 tsp. Vanilla Extract
2 cups All-purpose Flour
2-1/4 tsp. Baking Powder
1/2 tsp. Salt
3/4 cups Whole Milk
2 cups Fresh Blueberries

Topping:
3/4 sticks Butter
1/2 cup Sugar
1/2 tsp. Cinnamon (*if can tolerate*)
1/2 cup Flour
1/4 tsp. Salt

Preheat oven to 350 degrees. Combine flour, baking powder, and a salt. Stir and set aside. Cream 1/2 stick plus 1 tbsp. butter with cinnamon and sugar. Add egg and mix until combined. Add vanilla and mix. Add flour mixture and milk alternately until totally incorporated. Do not overbeat. Stir in blueberries until evenly distributed.

Grease a 9 x 13 inch baking pan. Pour in batter. In a separate bowl, combine topping ingredients and cut together using two knives or a pastry cutter. Sprinkle over the top of the cake. Bake cake for 40 to 45 minutes, or until golden brown. Sprinkle with sugar. Cut into squares and serve with softened butter.

## Italian Cream Cake (Carole)

*Buttermilk and Walnuts are on the try it list.*

Cake:
1 stick butter
1 cup vegetable oil
1 cup sugar
5 whole eggs, separated
3 tsp. vanilla
1 cup coconut (nitrate free)
2 cups all-purpose flour
1 tsp. baking soda
1 tsp. baking powder
1 cup buttermilk (if can tolerate)

Preheat oven to 350 degrees. Grease and flour three 9-inch round cake pans. Beat egg whites until stiff. Set aside.

In a large bowl, cream together butter, oil, and sugar until light and fluffy. Mix in the egg yolks, vanilla, and coconut. In a separate bowl, mix flour, baking soda, and baking powder. Alternate adding buttermilk and dry ingredients to wet ingredients. Mix until just combined, then fold in egg whites.

Pour evenly into the three prepared pans, then sprinkle the top of each pan with 1 (at least) tbsp. sugar. Bake in preheated oven for 20 to 25 minutes, or until toothpick comes out clean. Remove from oven and allow to cool for 15 minutes, then turn the cakes out onto cooling racks and allow to cool completely.

Frosting:
2 packages (8 oz.) cream cheese
1 stick butter
2 tsp. vanilla
1 package 2 lb. powdered sugar
1 cup chopped walnuts (*if can tolerate*)
1 cup sweetened, flaked coconut (*nitrate free*)

In a medium bowl, combine cream cheese, butter, vanilla, and powdered sugar. Beat until light and fluffy. Stir in chopped walnuts and sugared coconut. Spread between layers and serve.

*Cream cheese frosting will soften at room temperature, so refrigerate if you won't use it right away.*

## Tres Leches Cake (Carole)

*This is a really delicious cake!*

1 cup all-purpose flour
1 ½ tsp. baking powder
¼ tsp. salt
5 whole eggs
1 cup sugar, divided
1 tsp. vanilla
⅓ cup milk
1 can evaporated milk
1 can sweetened, condensed milk
¼ cup heavy cream

Icing:
1 pint heavy cream, for whipping
3 tbsp. sugar

Preheat oven to 350F. Spray a 9" x 13" pan liberally until coated. Combine flour, baking powder, and salt in a large bowl. Separate eggs. Beat egg yolks with ¾ cup sugar on high speed until yolks are pale yellow. Stir in milk and vanilla. Pour egg yolk mixture over the flour mixture and stir very gently until combined. Beat egg whites on high speed until soft peaks form. With the mixer on, pour in remaining ¼ cup sugar and beat until egg whites are stiff but not dry. Fold egg white mixture into the batter very gently until just combined. Pour into prepared pan and spread to even out the surface. Bake for 35 to 45 minutes or until a toothpick comes out clean. Turn cake out onto a rimmed platter and allow to cool.

Combine condensed milk, evaporated milk, and heavy cream in a small pitcher. When cake is cool, pierce the surface with a fork several times. Slowly drizzle all but about 1 cup of the milk mixture. Try to get as much around the edges of the cake as you can. Allow the cake to absorb the milk mixture for 30 minutes. To ice the cake, whip 1 pint heavy cream with 3 tbsp. of sugar until thick and spreadable. Spread over the surface of the cake. Decorate cake with whole or chopped organic maraschino cherries. Cut into squares and serve.

## Sweet Potato Cheesecake (Carole)

1 medium sweet potato
1 package cream cheese
½ can condensed milk
¾ cup brown sugar
¾ cup sugar
1 tsp. vanilla
2 medium eggs
graham cracker crusts (9" each)

Mix together and pour into crusts. Place into a preheated oven at 375F and cook for 55 minutes or until light brown.

## White Chocolate Banana Cake (carole)

½ cup shortening
2 cups sugar
2 eggs
1 ½ cups mashed ripe bananas (about 3 medium) If can tolerate
3 tsp. vanilla extract
3 cups all-purpose flour
1 tsp. baking powder
½ tsp. baking soda
½ tsp. salt
1 cup buttermilk (if can tolerate)
4 oz. white baking chocolate, melted and cooled

In a large bowl, cream shortening and sugar until light and fluffy. Add eggs, one at a time, beating will after each addition. Beat in bananas and vanilla. Combine the flour, baking powder, baking soda and salt. Add to creamed mixture alternately with buttermilk, beating well after each addition. Fold in chocolate.

Pour into three greased and floured 9" round baking pan. Bake at 350F for 25-30 minutes or until a toothpick inserted near the center comes out clean. Cool for 10 minutes before removing cake from pans to wire racks to cool completely.

Frosting:
1 package (8 oz.) cream cheese, softened
¾ cup butter, softened
1 tsp. vanilla extract
5 cups icing sugar

½ cup finely chopped nuts as desired and/or tolerated (toasted pecans are nice if can tolerate)

In a large bowl, beat the cream cheese, butter and vanilla until smooth. Gradually beat in icing sugar. Spread between layers and over top and sides of cake. Sprinkle with nuts.

*Note: Instead of nuts you can drizzle caramel sauce and/or melted white chocolate or sprinkle IC friendly shredded coconut.*

## Coconut Peach Cake (Carole)

*For those of us who can tolerate peaches. It's made like an upside down cake.*

6 tbsp. butter
⅔ cup brown sugar
1 tbsp. light corn syrup
1 ⅓ cups flaked coconut (make sure IC friendly nitrate free)
1 can (16 oz.) peach slices (make sure IC friendly)
1 cup sifted all-purpose flour (sift before measuring)
¾ cup granulated sugar
1 ¼ tsp. baking powder
¼ tsp. salt
¼ cup shortening
1 egg
½ cup milk
½ tsp. vanilla

Melt 6 tbsp. butter in an 8-inch square baking pan. Stir in brown sugar, corn syrup, and coconut. Pat to evenly cover bottom and up sides of pan. Arrange peach halves or slices, cut side up, over coconut. In a medium mixing bowl, sift together the sifted flour, granulated sugar, baking powder, and salt. Add remaining ingredients and blend on low speed of electric mixer. Increase mixer speed to medium and beat for 2 minutes. Spread batter over peaches.

Bake at 375F for 40 minutes, or until a wooden pick or cake tester inserted in center comes out with no cake batter clinging. Cool in pan for a minute or two before turning out onto serving plate. Serve warm, with whipped topping or ice cream if desired.

## Carrot Cake (Carole)

*I was sitting at work today and I was obviously hungry because all of a sudden I thought I want carrot cake. So here is the recipe for all of you to enjoy also. I think I need to finish eating the coconut cake with coconut cream frosting first before I make the carrot cake or I won't be able to fit in my chair.*

4 eggs
1 ¼ cups vegetable oil
2 cups white sugar
2 tsp. vanilla extract
2 cups all-purpose flour
2 tsp. baking soda
2 tsp. baking powder
½ tsp. salt
2 tsp. ground cinnamon *(if can tolerate)*
3 cups grated carrots
1 cup chopped nuts of your choice *(can be omitted)*

Preheat oven to 350 F (175C). Grease and flour a 9" x 13" inch pan. In a large bowl, beat together eggs, oil, white sugar and 2 tsp. vanilla. Mix in flour, baking soda, baking powder, salt and cinnamon. Stir in carrots. Fold in nuts. Pour into prepared pan.  Bake in the preheated oven for 40 to 50 minutes, or until a toothpick inserted into the center of the cake comes out clean. Let cool in pan for 10 minutes, then turn out onto a wire rack and cool completely.

Frosting
½ cup butter, softened
8 oz. cream cheese, softened
4 cups confectioners' sugar
1 tsp. vanilla extract

In a medium bowl, combine butter, cream cheese, confectioners' sugar and 1 tsp. vanilla. Beat until the mixture is smooth and creamy. Can add nuts to frosting if desired. Frost the cooled cake.

## White Chocolate Pound Cake (Diane M)

1 cup evaporated milk
4 oz. white chocolate
1 cup butter *(softened)*
1 ⅔ cups sugar
5 eggs
2 ¾  cups flour
½ tsp. baking soda
½ tsp. salt

Combine evaporated milk and white chocolate, stir over low heat until melted. Cool to room temperature. Cream butter and sugar. Add eggs one at a time, beating well. Combine flour, soda and salt. Add to the creamed mixture alternately with the white chocolate mixture. Beat just until combined. Pour into a greased and floured 10" tube pan. Bake at 325F for 1 hour or until a toothpick comes out clean.

Icing
3 oz. white chocolate
¼ cup butter (no substitutes)
2 cups confectioners sugar
½ tsp. vanilla
1 to 2 tbsp. milk

Melt white chocolate and butter over low heat until smooth, stirring often. Remove from heat and stir in confectioners sugar, vanilla and enough milk to reach desired consistency. Drizzle over cake.

## PIE

### Caramel Pie (Carole)

4 oz. cream cheese, softened
½ cup sweetened condensed milk
1 carton (8oz) frozen whipped topping, thawed
1 graham cracker crust (9 inches)
½ cup caramel ice cream topping
¾ cup coconut, toasted *(nitrate free)*
¼ cup chopped pecans, toasted *(if can tolerate)*

In a small bowl, beat cream cheese and milk until smooth. Fold in whipped topping. Spread half into pie crust. Drizzle with half of the caramel topping. Combine coconut and pecans. Sprinkle half over caramel topping. Repeat layers. Chill until serving.

## Oatmeal Pie (Carole)

3 eggs, beaten
1 cup light corn syrup
4 tbsp. butter
1 cup rolled oats *(non instant)*
½ cup brown sugar
¾ cup coconut *(nitrate free)*
½ cup walnuts or pecans *(as tolerated)*
2 tsp. vanilla extract
2 tbsp. all-purpose flour
1 (9") deep dish pie crust

Beat eggs with whisk. Add remaining ingredients and mix well. Pour into pie shell. Bake at 350F for 40 minutes, increase heat to 375F and bake for 10 more minutes. Let cool before cutting. Enjoy!

*Can add IC friendly apples or raisins as tolerated.*

## Easy Pumpkin Pie Ice Cream or Ice Cream Pie (wheresmysmokes)

I love pumpkin! Everything pumpkin. Pumpkin ice cream, custard, pumpkin rolls, etc! I could go on, but I'd sound like Bubba from Forrest Gump. Since the IC started, I haven't been able to eat pumpkin without flaring. I narrowed it down to what's ever in pumpkin pie spice, nutmeg, cloves, etc. I don't know which spice and I'm not about to try last night.

So I headed off to the store last night and got myself some Vanilla Bean ice cream. I scooped out about 1 cup into a regular cereal bowl. I let it melt to make it easier for mixing. Don't do this unless you want to make a milkshake, which is also a good idea. Then I put a few scoops of pumpkin puree in and mixed it up. I tasted it then added more until I liked it. Then I poured a lot of cinnamon into it, tasting it as I poured. It was missing something. I sprinkled some brown sugar on it. And then the final ingredient. I crushed up some snickerdoodle cookies and mixed those in. You could also just leave them on top. Absolutely delicious!!!

My mom does the first few steps, but instead of adding cookies, she pours the mixture into a graham cracker crust and then puts it in the freezer. So two very easy desserts for the fall or all year round, if you're like me.

## Eggnog Pumpkin Pie (Carole)

1 can (15 oz.) solid-pack pumpkin
1 ¼ cups eggnog
⅔ cup sugar
3 eggs
1 tsp. cinnamon *(if can tolerate)*
½ tsp. nutmeg *(if can tolerate)*
¼ tsp. ginger *(if can tolerate)*
¼ tsp. salt
1 unbaked pastry shell (9")

In a large bowl, combine the pumpkin, eggnog, sugar, eggs, spices and salt. Pour into pastry shell. Bake at 375F for 60-65 minutes or until a knife inserted near the center comes out clean. Cool on a wire rack. Refrigerate until serving.

## Angel Food Pie (Diane M)

baked pie shell *(can be graham cracker)*
4 ½ tbsp. cornstarch
¾ cup sugar
1 ½ cups boiling water
½ tsp. salt
3 egg whites
3 tbsp. sugar
1 tsp. vanilla
½ cup cream, whipped & sweetened or whipped topping
chopped nuts

Beat egg whites & salt until stiff. Add 3 tbsp. sugar & the vanilla. Beat until creamy. In a 1-qt. glass measure heat water in microwave for 2 minutes. Blend together cornstarch and ¾ cup sugar. Gradually stir into hot water. Heat in microwave another 1 ½ to 2 minutes, stirring every 30 seconds, until thickened. Pour slowly over egg whites, beating as you pour. Cool slightly then fill crust. Chill at least 2 hours. Cover with whipped cream, then sprinkle with nuts. (This recipe makes a very high 8-or 9-inch pie or two shallow pies.)

## Frozen Blueberry Cream Sandwiches (Blazer)

*This frozen dessert is delicious.*

1 small container of thawed Cool Whip® or homemade whip cream
1 pack cinnamon graham crackers
blueberries

In a mixing bowl, stir container Cool Whip® with blueberries. Lay out half of graham crackers. Put a generous amount of mixture onto each graham cracker.  Top each one with remaining crackers and smash down just enough to make a sandwich. Place sandwiches in freezer bags individually. Freeze overnight and enjoy!

## Fruit Cobbler (Diane M)

2 cups fresh blueberries *(any IC friendly fruit will do)*
1 cup all-purpose flour
2 tsp. baking powder
1 cup sugar
2 eggs
¾ cup milk
1 tsp. vanilla extract
1 tsp. grated lemon rind *(if can tolerate)*
Whipped cream or vanilla ice cream *(optional)*

Wash and dry the berries if using fresh, or thaw, drain and dry the frozen berries. Place in the bottom of a 2 quart ovenproof casserole or souffle dish. Sift the flour and baking powder into a large mixing bowl. Add the sugar, eggs, milk, vanilla, and lemon rind. Mix with a wooden spoon until thoroughly combined. Pour the batter over the berries and bake in the center of a 350F (180C) oven for one hour, until the top is browned. Remove from oven and let cool at least 15 minutes before serving. Top individual portions with whipped cream or vanilla ice cream if desired. Serves 4 to 6.

## Baked Indian Pudding (Diane M)

3 cups milk
3 tbsp. yellow cornmeal
½ cup dark molasses *(if can tolerate)*
1 egg

½ cup sugar
1 tbsp. melted butter
½ tsp. ground ginger *(if can tolerate)*
½ tsp. cinnamon *(if can tolerate)*

Preheat oven to 300F. Heat milk in saucepan when it comes to a boil, gradually stir in cornmeal, using wire whisk. Cook stirring constantly, until slightly thickened. Stir in molasses. Beat egg in a large mixing bowl and add sugar, butter, ginger, cinnamon and salt. Pour in hot mixture stirring rapidly. When blended, pour the mixture into a greased baking dish. Bake for one hour or until knife comes out clean.

## Fried Coconut Puffs (Carole)

1 cup sifted flour
1 tbsp.. coconut oil
½ tsp. salt
¼ cup plus 1 tbsp. water

Sift dry ingredients together and add water. Mix well with your hands for about 5 minutes. The more you mix it, the more they will puff. Pinch off balls about the size of a walnut. Roll each one on a floured board to a circle about 4 inches.

Filling:
1 c. shredded coconut
½ c. sugar
2 tbsp.. water
1 tsp. cinnamon *(if can tolerate)*

Mix together and cook over low heat until sugar is dissolved. Put tsp. of filling on circle, fold in half, dampen edges, and press tightly together. This is important so filling does not come out while frying. Fry in hot coconut oil in a deep-fryer or wok at 375F (190C) until lightly browned. Drain on absorbent paper. Makes 12 or more.

## Mint White Chocolate Mousse (Carole)

6 oz. chopped premium white chocolate
1 ¼ cups whipping cream, divided
2 egg whites
⅛ tsp. cream of tartar
2 tsp. granulated sugar

2 tsp. vanilla extract
Few drops mint extract

In a large bowl over (but not touching) simmering water, slowly melt your 6 oz. white chocolate with ¼ cup cream, stirring occasionally. Set aside to cool to lukewarm for about 15 minutes. While it's cooling, beat the remaining whipping cream with sugar, vanilla, and mint extract until peaks form. Set aside.

In another large bowl, with dry and clean beaters, whip the egg whites with cream of tartar until stiff peaks form but eggs are not dry. Gently fold the egg whites into the now-cooled chocolate mixture until just combined. Gently fold in the whipping cream until just combined. Caution: do not re-whip this or the texture will become granular. Dish the mousse.

### Coffee Break Treat (Blazer)

1 can crescent rolls
1 or 2 Fuji apples
handful of mint leaves *(optional)*
2 tbsp. melted butter
1 tbsp. cinnamon and 1 tbsp. of sugar mixed together in bowl

Lay out crescent rolls on cookie sheet. Slice apple into equal slices (enough for each roll). Roll up an apple slice and a mint leaf into each piece of dough starting at the wider end of the triangle. Brush each one with butter. Sprinkle each one with Cinnamon and sugar. Bake 12 minutes or until golden brown at 350F.

# COOKIES

### Cashew Butter Cookies (Clevsea)

1 cup sugar
1 cup brown sugar
½ up butter
½ cup melted coconut oil
1 egg
1 cup cashew butter
3 cups flour---mixed (or sifted) with 1 tsp. baking soda, and ½ tsp. salt

Mix the sugars, the butter, the coconut oil until combined and add 1 egg. Then add the cashew butter. In a separate bowl mix the flour, baking soda and salt. Then add the dry ingredients to the wet. Roll into balls. Flatten with a fork dipped in flour. 375 degrees for 6 to 10 minutes. until set, not brown. Un-greased pan.

*They are great! Make extra and after they are cooked and cooled store them in a "Freezer" style baggie in the freezer. Instant cookie ready when you want it!!*

### Snowball Cookies (wcrox)

1 cup butter, softened
½ cup powdered sugar
1 tsp. vanilla
2 ¼ cups flour
¼ tsp. salt
¾ cup finely chopped nuts (pecans, walnuts, or almonds)
Powdered sugar for rolling

Preheat oven to 375F. Line two cookie sheets with parchment paper. Mix butter, ½ cup powdered sugar, and vanilla with an electric mixer until fluffy. Add flour and salt and mix until the dough comes together. Stir in the nuts. If dough is too soft, chill it until you can work it easily with your hands.

Scoop 1 tbsp. balls of dough and place on prepared cookie sheet. Bake cookies for 7-8 minutes until bottoms are just slightly brown. Remove from oven and cool for just a minute, until you can handle them. Fill a small bowl with powdered sugar and roll each cookie in the sugar until coated. Place on a rack to cool. Once cookies are cooled, you may want to re-roll them in more powdered sugar.

### Carob Brownies (emilyandlouise)

5 tbsp. carob powder
½ cup butter, softened
2 eggs
1 cup packed light brown sugar
½ cup almonds, processed into a fine meal
¼ cup rice flour
½ tsp. sea salt
¼ tsp. baking soda
2 tsp. vanilla extract

Preheat the oven to 350F. Grease and 8" x 8" pan. In a bowl combine the dry ingredients and whisk. In a bowl, combine the wet ingredients and mix. Add the wet to the dry ingredients and mix until combined. The batter will be thick. Spread into the greased pan. Add crushed almonds on top.

Bake in 350F oven for 33-35 minutes . Do not over bake! Cool in pan on a wire rack. Remove from pan. Chill before cutting so they don't break apart. (I ate them warm out of the pan.)

## Butterscotch Brownies (Diane M)

¼ cup shortening or butter
1 cup light brown sugar *(packed)*
1 egg
¾ cup sifted flour
1 tsp. baking powder
½ tsp. salt
½ tsp. vanilla
¾ cup butterscotch chips

Heat oven to 350F. Melt butter over low heat. Remove from heat and blend in brown sugar. Cool. Stir in egg. Sift together and stir in flour, baking powder and salt. Stir in vanilla and chips. Spread in well-greased and floured square pan, 8" by 8" by 2". Bake 20-25 minutes until a light touch with finger leaves slight print. Cut into bars while warm. This is an old recipe and very good!

## Crunchy Cookies (Diane M)

2 cups unsifted flour
1 tsp. baking powder
1 tsp. baking soda
1 tsp. salt
1 cup butter
1 cup brown sugar
1 cup granulated sugar
2 eggs
2 ⅔ cups coconut
3 cups corn flake cereal (organic)
2 tsp. vanilla

Cream the butter and sugars together. Add the eggs and mix well. Mix the flour with the baking powder, baking soda and salt. Add the flour mixture to the butter/sugar mixture. Mix well. Add vanilla and mix well. Lastly, add the corn flake cereal and coconut and mix well.

Drop by teaspoons on an ungreased cookie sheet. Bake at 350F (180C) for 12 minutes. Cookies will look slightly underdone, but they brown a little after being taken from the oven. Make sure you take them from the oven before they look done; in other words, don't bake them until really browned. They'll lose their chewy texture!

## Peanut Butter Cookies Gluten Free (agilityme)

*One of my students baked these cookies for me and shared the recipe when I first went gluten free. They are still as good today as they were then. Hope you enjoy.*

2 cups peanut butter
1 cup brown sugar
1 cup white sugar
4 eggs, beaten
1 tsp. vanilla
1 ½ cups carob chips or 1 ½ cups chopped nuts *(optional)*

Preheat oven to 350F. Grease cookie sheet. Combine peanut butter, eggs, sugar and vanilla. Mix until smooth. Add carob chips or nuts if you are using them. Bake about 12 minutes or until lightly browned. Let the cookies cool on the cookie sheet before removing.

## Pear Custard Bars (Diane M)

½ cup butter
⅓ cup sugar
¾ cup flour
¼ tea. vanilla
⅔ cup nuts *(optional)*

Filling/Topping
1 package 8 oz. cream cheese softened
½ cup sugar
1 egg
½ tsp. vanilla
1 can (15 oz.) pear halves, drained
½ tsp. sugar

½ tsp. cinnamon *(if can tolerate)*

Cream butter and sugar. Beat in the flour and vanilla until combined. Add nuts. Press into a greased 8" square baking pan. Bake for 20 minutes or until lightly browned, at 350F. Beat cream cheese until smooth. Add sugar, egg and vanilla; mix until combined. Pour over crust. Cut pears into ⅛" slices. Arrange in a single layer over filling. Combine sugar and cinnamon. Sprinkle over pears. Bake at 375F for 28 to 30 minutes. Cool.

## Cake Batter Fudge (Carole)

1 cup organic yellow cake mix *(make sure IC friendly)*

1 cup confectioners sugar
½ stick (¼ cup) butter cut into small squares
¼ cup milk

Mix cake mix and icing sugar in microwave safe bowl. Add butter and milk. Don't stir. Microwave for 2 minutes. Stir immediately until completely combined. Spread into greased pan. Refrigerate for at least one hour.

*\*Makes one 6 x 6" container, or double for an 8 x 8" pan.*
*\*Notes: If the batter comes out too runny, stir in about 1 tsp. or sugar or cake mix at a time until stiff. If too thick to stir in all components, slowly add ½ tsp. of milk at a time, but batter should be thick!*

# Appendix A.

The purpose of the **2012 ICN Food List** is to give patients variety. Many mistakenly assume that they can only eat very few foods and, for the majority of patients, this is simply not true. We can usually eat quite a few foods but we have to choose carefully. Consider apples. Granny Smith apples, known for their tartness and acidity, are good baking apples but, for a sensitive bladder or prostate, are a bit too harsh. Gala and Fuji apples, however, are milder, sweeter, contain less acid and are much more bladder friendly. As you review this list, consider not only the types but also the varieties and brands of foods that you are eating. Your favorite brand from years ago may not work today because of the use of preservatives or acids. There's a good chance, though, that you'll find a new brand that does work well in your body today.

This list presents foods in three columns:

- "Bladder Friendly Foods" are those that most patients tolerate well. These are the foods and beverages we suggest that you consume when you are having bladder discomfort. They rarely trigger bladder irritation. Foods with a (+) sign can be soothing during an IC flare.

- "Foods Worth Trying Cautiously" are generally safe though they may irritate more sensitive bladders. They should be tried in small quantities first.

- "Foods to Avoid" are those well known for triggering bladder discomfort.

You should be able to tolerate most of the bladder friendly foods unless you have profound bladder wall damage, food sensitivities or intolerances. Of course, there may be a few on this list that you don't quite work for you. Just cross them out and work on creating your own preferred food list. Most patients can tolerate many of the foods in the second column and we encourage you to try them in small quantities first and see how you do.

Foods in the third column are usually problematic for most patients and should be avoided. Cranberries, for example, are known as the "acid bomb" in IC circles for their high acidity and tendency to cause bladder irritation and pain. Yes, beer lovers may miss their Guinness® but there's a substantial chance that it could trigger more discomfort. It's best to stay with the lighter beers and lagers.

If we've missed any foods or you would like an opinion on a food, please send us an email at: jill@ic-network.com

| | Usually Bladder Friendly | Foods Worth Trying | Foods To Avoid |
|---|---|---|---|
| **Acacia Fiber** | powdered, unflavored | | |
| **Acidophilous** | acidophilous capsules | | |
| **Allspice** | | ground or grated | |
| **Almond Extract** | look for organic, higher quality extracts | | |
| **Almonds** | unsalted, organic, raw, roasted or almond butter (i e Zinke & Blue Diamond) | lightly seasoned, candied, caramel or carob covered almonds (i e Nunes Farms) | chocolate covered, heavily seasoned with "hot" chili flavoring and spices |
| **Aloe** | | Desert Harvest Aloe® capsules | aloe beverages containing risky ingredients such as Vitamin C, Maca, Camu |
| **Amaranth** | | amaranth - grain, cereal | |
| **Anise** | ground & pods | | |
| **Apples** | sweet, mild apples (i e Gala, Fuji, Pink Lady), jam, jelly, pies, tarts, juice | sweet Red or Green Delicious apples | sour or very tart apples (i e Granny Smith) |
| **Applesauce** | homemade applesauce made with Gala, Fuji or Pink Lady apples | brand name or baby applesauces may include acids or spices that can irritate the bladder | |
| **Apricots** | | fresh apricots, jam, jelly, pies, tarts, organic dried apricots | |
| **Artichokes** | fresh, steamed & boiled | | artichoke hearts marinated in vinegar |
| **Ascorbic Acid** | | low acid ester C | ascorbic acid |
| **Asparagus** | fresh, steamed & boiled | | asparagus marinated in vinegar |
| **Autolyzed Yeast** | | | autolyzed yeast |
| **Avocado** | fresh, ice cream, mild guacamole | | guacamole with strong, hot, chili spices |
| **Bacon** | uncured, preservative free turkey or pork bacon | mildly spiced, cured bacon products | heavily cured, preserved, smoked or spiced bacon products |
| **Baking Powder & Soda** | double acting or single acting powder, baking soda | | |
| **Bananas** | | fresh banana, bread, fritters, ice cream | chocolate covered, banana chips treated with sulfur |
| **Basil** | fresh, flakes, infused olive oil | pesto sauce | |
| **Beans** | black eyed peas, garbanzo, lentils, pinto, white, most dried beans | fava, kidney beans, lima beans, black beans | |
| **Beef** | fresh or frozen roasts, steaks, ground beef & other cuts | mild corned beef | heavily spiced, preserved or prepackaged products |
| **Beer** | | light lagers, light hybrid beers, light ales | brown ales, stout, hard cider, german white or rye beer, belgian or french ale, brown ales |
| **Beets** | fresh, steamed, boiled, canned | | pickled beets in vinegar |
| **Bell Peppers** | yellow, orange and red peppers | green peppers | |
| **Berries** | blueberries | blackberries, raspberries, olallieberries | cranberries, strawberries in large quantities |
| **Blueberries** | jam, fruit bars, tarts and pies, ice cream | | |

| | Usually Bladder Friendly | Foods Worth Trying | Foods To Avoid |
|---|---|---|---|
| **Breads** | corn,+, oat+, pita, potato+, white+, Italian sweet, whole wheat | rye, pumpernickel, sourdough breads - Ezekiel bread is popular for its high fiber and protein but could bother soy sensitive patients | breads made with unsafe ingredients and/or heavily processed and fortified |
| **Breads - sweet** | homemade zucchini bread+, pumpkin bread, apple bread | banana bread | |
| **Broccoli** | fresh, frozen, steamed, boiled | | |
| **Brussels Sprouts** | fresh, frozen, steamed, boiled | | |
| **Butter and Margarine** | real butter, sweetened or unsweetened | Soybean oil based margarines may be irritating for some | |
| **Buttermilk** | | fresh - try a small amount first to see if you tolerate it well | |
| **Cabbage** | raw or cooked | | pickled or sauerkraut |
| **Cake** | homemade pound, angel food, white+, yellow+ | Dr Oetker's Organic White Cake Mix, carrot cake without problem ingredients | chocolate, commercial mixes that use artificial colorings and flavorings |
| **Calcium** | calcium citrate or carbonate tablets | | |
| **Candy** | carob, caramel, mint, butterscotch, divinity | licorice, white chocolate, cotton, mild gums (sugar or xylitol based) | red hot-type cinnamons, sour candy, most sugar-free candy and gums |
| **Cantaloupe** | | fresh - try in small quantities, it is more irritating than other melons | |
| **Caraway** | caraway seeds | | |
| **Carob** | chips, powder, candy | | |
| **Carrots** | fresh, raw or steamed | carrot cake without problem ingredients | |
| **Catsup and Ketchup** | | used in small quantities | used in large quantities |
| **Cauliflower** | fresh, raw or steamed | | |
| **Cayenne** | | | cayenne |
| **Celery** | fresh, raw or steamed | | |
| **Celery Seed** | | ground | |
| **Cereals** | oatmeal, oat, rice and fiber without problem ingredients | Ezekiel Cereal, Fiber-One, Kashi Go-Lean, Grape Nuts, Cheerios, Kashi Autumn Wheat | heavily preserved, sweetened, flavored, chocolate |
| **Cheese** | American, mozzarella, cheddar cheese (mild), feta, ricotta+, string cheeses+ | blue cheese, brie, brick parmesan, camembert, cheddar cheese (sharp), edam, emmenthaler, gruyere hard jack, Monterey Jack, parmesan (fresh & canned), Roquefort, stilton, Swiss | processed, heavily spiced, cheese in a can products |
| **Cheese Substitutes** | | | tofu and soy cheeses |
| **Cheesecake** | plain, vanilla bean, blueberry, peppermint, caramel, dulce de leche, pumpkin | dutch apple | chocolate, mocha, lemon, key lime, strawberry |
| **Cherimoya** | | fresh | |
| **Cherries** | | fresh cherries, organic maraschino | sour cherries |

| | Usually Bladder Friendly | Foods Worth Trying | Foods To Avoid |
|---|---|---|---|
| **Chervil** | | dried chervil | |
| **Chicken** | fresh cooked (baked, fried, roasted, sauteed) | | "fast food," prepackaged, heavily spiced chicken products |
| **Chili Peppers** | | | hot, chili pepper flakes, medium or hot salsa, "hot" spiced foods such as chili, bbq, hot wing sauce |
| **Chili Powder** | | | ground chili powder |
| **Chips** | corn or potato chips - plain | | strongly seasoned or salty chips, such as barbecue, buffalo wing, jalapeno, sweet chili, salt & vinegar, red hot, cheddar & sour cream |
| **Chives** | fresh, dried | | |
| **Chocolate** | carob is a bladder friendly substitute | white or a very high quality dark | milk, bittersweet, cocoa powder |
| **Cilantro** | | fresh, dried | |
| **Cinnamon** | | ceylon cinnamon | chinese cassia cinnamon may be too strong |
| **Citric acid** | | very small quantities when used as a preservative for some canned foods | large quantities or when used as a flavoring (i e  most sodas) |
| **Citrus Fruits** | | | lemons, limes, oranges, grapefruit, clementine |
| **Citrus Peel** | | fresh or dried citrus peel | candied citrus peels |
| **Cloves** | | | ground, whole |
| **Coconut** | flakes (untreated, organic), milk, ice cream, sorbet | | coconut treated with metabisulfite |
| **Coffees** | | herbal coffees (Pero, Cafix, Kaffree Roma) or low acid decaf coffees (Simpatico, Euromild, Puroast or Tyler's) | traditional coffees (regular & decaf) should be avoided due to their high acid and/or caffeine content |
| **Colonoscopy Preps** | MiraLAX® protocol with water | MiraLAX® protocol with clear, green or blue Gatorade® | |
| **Cookies** | oatmeal+ , shortbread, sugar+, carob chip, mexican wedding, biscotti, almond | snickerdoodles, peanut butter | chocolate chip, cranberry |
| **Coriander** | ground | | |
| **Corn** | fresh yellow, white, blue, mixed corn, cornmeal, polenta, grits | | |
| **Cottage Cheese** | plain cottage cheese, large curd made with sennet (low acid) | cottage cheese, small curd made without rennet (higher acid) | |
| **Crackers** | matzo, soda or soup | crackers without obvious problem ingredients, Triskets, organic, stone ground wheat, rice thins | strongly spiced crackers |
| **Cranberry Products** | | | all juice, supplements, pills |
| **Cream Cheese** | fresh, plain cream cheese | mildly spiced cream cheeses (i e pumpkin, italian herb, savory garlic) | |
| **Cucumber** | burpless hybrid, orient express or sweet slice varieties | | dill or sweet pickle relish and pickles may include vinegar |

| | Usually Bladder Friendly | Foods Worth Trying | Foods To Avoid |
|---|---|---|---|
| **Cumin** | | ground | |
| **Currants** | | organic fresh or dried currants | |
| **Curry - Hot** | | | curry powder, hot |
| **Custards** | vanilla, coconut, creme brulee | | |
| **Dates** | organic fresh or dried dates | | |
| **Deli Meats** | filler, gluten, color free meats (i.e. Boar's Head, Hormel Natural) | liverwurst, ham, bologna, mortadella, prosciutto without heavy preservatives or flavorings | heavily spiced, salted, flavored meat products such as salami and pepperoni |
| **Dill** | fresh, dried | | |
| **Divinity** | vanilla, peppermint | | |
| **Donuts** | glazed, sugar coated, old fashioned, cream cheese | maple, apple, raspberry | chocolate |
| **Dried Fruit** | | organic dried apples, peaches, apricots, prunes without preservatives | dried fruits with preservatives |
| **Drink Powders** | | white hot chocolate mixes | Kool-aid®, lemonade, orange, and all powdered chocolate and sweet tea drinks |
| **Eggnog** | fresh eggnog without alcohol | | eggnog with coffee or strong alcohol |
| **Eggplant** | baked, sauteed | | eggplant parmigiana with tomato sauce |
| **Eggs** | artificial-stimulant-free and veggie-fed eggs, dried or pasteurized egg whites | Egg Beaters | |
| **Fennel** | fennel - fresh, dried | | |
| **Fibers** | bulk acacia fiber (Heather's Tummy Fiber™), bulk psyllium fiber (Benefiber®, Metamucil Clear & Natural®) - psyllium or inulin without artificial sugars or citrus flavors | Metamucil® Cinnamon Wafers | Metamucil® - orange, lemon or berry  Benefiber® - Plus Heart Health, Plus Calcium contain artificial sugar and orange flavoring |
| **Figs** | | fresh, dried | |
| **Fish** | fresh or frozen cod, sole, tilapia, salmon, tuna, anchovies | canned tuna, salmon, anchovies or caviar packed in water | "fast food," heavily spiced, smoked, preserved or prepackaged products |
| **Fish Oil** | capsules, liquid without citrus | | fish oils using lemon or other citrus flavors |
| **Flax Seed Oil** | | capsules | |
| **Flours** | buckwheat, wheat, rice, corn | | soy |
| **Folic Acid** | | tablets | |
| **Frostings** | homemade vanilla, buttercream, caramel, carob frostings and whipped cream | Dr  Oetker's Organic Vanilla Frosting Mix | most canned frostings contain high amounts of preservatives, sweeteners and artificial flavorings |
| **Fruit & Nut Bars** | blueberry, pear | almond, peanut, coconut, apple, blueberry, raisin | cranberry, tart grape, chocolate |
| **Fruitcakes** | | | whiskey, alcohol, rum, risky dried fruits, risky nuts |
| **Garden/Veggie Burgers** | | fresh, preservative free garden burgers - beware soy sauce | soy veggie patties |

| | Usually Bladder Friendly | Foods Worth Trying | Foods To Avoid |
|---|---|---|---|
| | | flavoring | |
| Garlic | fresh, dried, powder, infused oil | garlic salt | |
| Ginger | | fresh, dried | |
| Graham Crackers | organic, plain, honey coated | cinnamon | |
| Grapes | | fresh, sweet grapes | tart or bitter grapes |
| Green Beans | fresh, frozen | canned beans | |
| Greens | collard greens, kale, mustard greens, okra, swiss chard, spinach, bok choy | chicory, dandelion greens, purslane, turnip greens | |
| Guava | | | fresh or preserved guava products |
| Gum | sugar based, mint or licorice flavors | sweetened with xylitol, mint or licorice flavors | gums with most artificial sweeteners, hot spicy flavors, citrus flavors |
| Horseradish | | | grated, flakes, powder |
| Hot Dogs | uncured, preservative free chicken, turkey, beef or pork hot dogs (i e Niman Ranch) | mildly seasoned hot dogs | cured, smoked hot dogs |
| Hydrolyzed Protein | | | hydrolyzed protein may be hidden MSG |
| Ice Cream | peppermint, vanilla+ | caramel, coconut, mango, peppermint, almond, butter pecan | chocolate, coffee, rocky road, citrus flavors |
| Italian Sodas | blueberry, coconut, pear made with low sodium mineral water | raspberry, blackberry, strawberry, root beer, peach, watermelon | cola, lemon, lime, orange, chocolate, coffee using high sodium mineral waters |
| Juices | blueberry & pear  (i.e. Knudsen's Organic Pear juice) | baby apple or grape juices, low acid orange juice, some "organic" adult apple juices | cranberry, grapefruit, regular orange, tomato and acai juices |
| Kiwi fruit | | | fresh or preserved kiwi fruit, jams and jelly |
| Lamb | fresh or frozen | | heavily spiced, preserved or prepacked lamb products |
| Lard | lard | | |
| Leeks | | fresh, usually cooked | |
| Lemon extract | | organic, lemon extract | |
| Lettuce & Salad Greens | green leafy, romaine, butterhead, iceberg, looseleaf | bitter salad greens (i e  radicchio) | |
| Licorice | | black, raspberry, cherry licorice | |
| Liquors & Spirits | | sake, scotch, brandy, bourbon, gin, rum, vodka | whiskey, liqueurs, tequila |
| Liver | beef or chicken liver | | |
| Mace | ground | | |
| Malt Powder | | preservative free | |
| Mango | | fresh or dried mango, juice, jams and jellies | |
| Maple Syrup | homemade or store bought authentic maple syrup | | all imitation syrups - regular, lite or sugar free |

| | Usually Bladder Friendly | Foods Worth Trying | Foods To Avoid |
|---|---|---|---|
| **Marjoram** | fresh, dried+ | | |
| **Mayonnaise** | | regular and olive oil mayonnaise | |
| **Meat Tenderizers** | | | these usually contain MSG and high salt |
| **Melons** | | crenshaw, honeydew, watermelon | cantaloupe |
| **Milk** | regular, low fat, non-fat, lactaid | goat's milk | chocolate, soy |
| **Milk Substitutes** | almond and rice milks | regular non-dairy creamers, such as Mocha Mix | soybean based, chocolate or mocha flavors |
| **Milkshakes** | vanilla, coconut and caramel are usually bladder friendly | blueberry, peach or other IC friendly fruits | chocolate, coffee and mocha shakes |
| **Miso** | | | powder, liquid |
| **Mixers** | water, low acid sparkling water (San Pellegrino), milk, cream, egg nog | blueberry juice, peach juice, pomegranate juice, apple juice, root beer | lime juice, lemon juice, lemonade, cola, lemon sodas, tomato juice |
| **MSG & Misc. Additives** | | | monosodium glutamate, modified food starch, hydrolyzed proteins, sodium caseinate, yeast extract, autolyzed yeast |
| **Muffins** | oatmeal, carrot, bran, apple, corn, pumpkin, blueberry | cinnamon, raspberry, blackberry, banana | chocolate, chocolate chip, cranberry, orange, lemon poppyseed |
| **Mushrooms** | button, chantarelle, shiitake, portabello, enoki, truffles | | |
| **Mustard** | | mild, sweet flavors | hot, spicy, alcohol infused flavors |
| **Nectarines** | | fresh, very sweet nectarines | sour or tart nectarines |
| **Non-Dairy Creamers** | creamers without soybean oil | Mocha Mix® for patients not sensitive to soy | artificially flavored creamers, such as coffee, chocolate, mocha or cherry |
| **Noodles & Pasta** | wheat, rice, corn, quinoa | pesto, carbonara, clam, alfredo | tomato, premade pasta dishes with heavy flavorings and/or preservatives |
| **Nut Butters** | almond, peanut that are lower in salt and hydrogenated oils (i e Zinke Farms) | | |
| **Nutmeg** | | ground | |
| **Nuts** | almonds, cashews, peanuts | macadamia, pecans, walnuts | filberts, hazelnuts, pecans, pistachios |
| **Oatmeal Bars** | oatmeal bars without problem ingredients | | chocolate, cranberry |
| **Oils** | almond, canola, coconut, corn, olive, peanut, safflower, sesame, herb infused olive oils | Soybean oil can bother some patients  Try it cautiously! | |
| **Olives** | black olives in water | green olives in water, green olives stuffed with almonds | martini olives marinated in vermouth or stuffed with chili peppers |
| **Onion Powder** | | organic white, yellow, red, toasted | |
| **Onions** | | white, red, green, pearl, scallions, chives | raw bulb onions |
| **Orange Extract** | | organic extract in very small quantities | |
| **Oregano** | fresh, dried | | |

87

| | Usually Bladder Friendly | Foods Worth Trying | Foods To Avoid |
|---|---|---|---|
| **Papaya** | | fresh or preserved papaya products | |
| **Paprika** | | made from bell peppers | made from chili peppers, oleoresin paprika |
| **Parsley** | fresh or dried | | |
| **Passion Fruit** | | fresh or preserved products, juice | |
| **Pastries** | plain, almond, pear, custard, pumpkin | blueberry, cinnamon | chocolate and/or problem fruits |
| **Peaches** | | fresh peaches, jam, pie, tart, juice | |
| **Peanut Butter** | organic, natural peanut butters that are lower in salt and hydrogenated oils | | |
| **Peanuts** | raw, roasted, unsalted, lightly salted, peanut butter | | heavily spiced, salted, or coated with chocolate |
| **Pears** | juice, fruit bars, jams, canned pears in pear juice | | |
| **Peas** | green peas+, snow peas, split peas (fresh or dried) | | |
| **Pepper** | fresh | black, white, green powders | cayenne, pink, sichuan powders |
| **Persimmon** | | persimmon fruit | |
| **Pickles** | | | sweet or dill |
| **Pie** | custard, cream pie, homemade apple pie (with safe apples), pumpkin pie | peach pie, banana cream | pecan, mincemeat, key lime, lemon meringue, chocolate |
| **Pineapple** | | | pineapple fruit and juice |
| **Pizza** | plain, mild cheese, mushroom, veggie made without red sauce | plain, chicken & garlic, veggie, ham, alfredo sauce, creamy garlic sauce, basil pesto sauce | pepperoni, hot sausage, marinara sauce, bbq sauce, chili pepper flakes |
| **Plums** | | fresh, sweet, organic dried plums & prunes | |
| **Popcorn** | homemade (fried or steamed) | "all natural" microwaveable popcorn with no added flavors, preservatives or colors | microwaveable packages heavily spiced (i e  jalapeno, kettle corn, spicy nacho, etc ) |
| **Poppy Seed** | poppy seeds, muffins, cakes | | |
| **Popsicles** | coconut, vanilla, carob | banana, blueberry, mango and raspberry | chocolate, lemon, orange, lime |
| **Pork** | fresh or frozen | uncured, preservative free hot dogs, bacon and sausage (i e Niman Ranch products) | heavily spiced, preserved or cured pork products |
| **Potato Flakes** | dried | | |
| **Potatoes** | white, red, yellow, baking, sweet, yams | | |
| **Preservatives** | | | BHA, BHT, benzoates, citric acid, metabisulfite, sulfite |
| **Pretzels** | plain, unsalted | lightly salted | heavily spiced or salted |
| **Prosciutto** | | mild with minimal preservatives | |
| **Protein Powder** | whey, egg whites (i e  Just White's Egg White Powder) | | soy powders |
| **Prunes** | fresh plums | organic dried prunes, prune juice (diluted with water) | avoid heavily preserved dried fruit |

| | Usually Bladder Friendly | Foods Worth Trying | Foods To Avoid |
|---|---|---|---|
| **Psyllium Fiber** | ground, coarse (husk) | | sugar free or citrus flavored psyllium fiber products |
| **Puddings** | tapioca, vanilla+, rice+, coconut, creme brulee | butterscotch, banana | chocolate |
| **Pumpkin** | fresh, canned, soup, bread, muffins without problem ingredients | | |
| **Quinoa** | flour, pasta, bread, cereal | | |
| **Radishes** | fresh | | |
| **Raisins** | | organic, untreated gold or brown | treated gold or brown |
| **Red Wines** | none | Merlot, Pinot noir, Cabernet, Syrah | Sangiovese, Zinfandel, Port |
| **Rhubarb** | fresh | | strawberry & rhubarb pie |
| **Rice** | short grain, long grain, basmati, wild | | cajun, spicy boxed products |
| **Rice Dream®** | vanilla | carob almond, mint carob chip | chocolate |
| **Rosemary** | fresh, dried | | |
| **Rutabaga** | fresh, organic | | |
| **Sage** | sage+ fresh, dried | | |
| **Salad Dressing** | some homemade salad dressings (i e ranch dressing), herb Infused olive oils | "organic" brand name dressings without problem ingredients or spices (i.e. Marie's) | oil & vinegar, dressings with strong "hot" spices |
| **Salt** | table, sea, iodized, kosher, celtic in small quantities | coarse in small quantities | rock, seasoned |
| **Sauerkraut** | | | sauerkraut, pickled cabbage |
| **Sausages** | uncured, preservative free chicken, pork or turkey sausages | mildly spiced sausage or sausage meat, such as mild italian sausage or breakfast sausages | avoid heavily preserved, cured, smoked or spiced sausages |
| **Seafood** | clams, crabmeat (not canned), lobster, shrimp | | heavily spiced, preserved or prepacked seafood products, canned crab meat |
| **Seeds** | | organic, unsalted or lightly salted sunflower, pumpkin, sesame seeds | heavily seasoned, hot spiced, salty |
| **Senna** | | | teas, pills |
| **Sherbet** | vanilla, coconut, peppermint | raspberry, blackberry, melon, mango, strawberry | chocolate or citrus flavors |
| **Shortening** | shortenings free of soybean oil | Soybean oil based products | |
| **Smoked Fish** | | | heavily preserved, salted and/or cured smoked fish |
| **Snack Cakes** | homemade vanilla, pound or carrot cakes | | fast food snack cakes |
| **Soft Drinks & Sodas** | | caffeine free root beer with ice may be attempted once or twice a month | all colas, sugar or diet, energy drinks, all citrus, mountain, ginger, guarana, strawberry |
| **Sorbet** | blueberry, pear, coconut | raspberry, blackberry, mango, peach | lemon, lime, orange |
| **Soups - Bouillon** | homemade chicken, beef or vegetable bouillon or stock | | bouillon cubes, powder |
| **Soups - Canned** | | organic and/or reduced salt canned soups | brand name soups high in salt and/or have problem ingredients |

| | Usually Bladder Friendly | Foods Worth Trying | Foods To Avoid |
|---|---|---|---|
| Soups - Homemade | homemade chicken, beef, turkey, squash, pea, bean, carrot, potato, corn | | tomato soup, minestrone made with heavy tomato sauce, hot chili |
| Soups - Packaged | | | most instant or prepackaged soups |
| Sour Cream | | sour cream | |
| Soy Beans | | | edamame, roasted |
| Soy Products | | fresh, unflavored tofu | soy veggie patties, flour protein powder, aged tofu |
| Soy Sauce | | | soy sauce |
| Specialty Grains | couscous, grits, millet, quinoa+, spelt | amaranth | |
| Squash | summer (zucchini, patty pan, crookneck, yellow) winter (acorn, butternut, patty pan, spaghetti) | | |
| Starfruit | | fresh | |
| Stool Softeners | polyethylene glycol products - Miralax® | docusate products | |
| Strawberries | | fresh, sweet strawberries (in small quantities) | strawberries in large quantities, sour strawberries, jams, jellies, flavorings |
| Sweeteners - Artificial | | Splenda® (sucralose), Truvia® (stevia) | acesulfame K, aspartame, Nutrasweet®, saccharine, Sweet-N-Low® |
| Sweeteners+ | brown sugar, white sugar, honey+ | Splenda® (sucralose), Truvia® (stevia) | acesulfame K, aspartame, Nutrasweet®, saccharine, Sweet-N-Low®, Stevia |
| Tahini | | tahini sauce in a small quantity | |
| Tamari | | | tamari sauce |
| Tarragon | fresh, dried | | |
| Teas | chamomile+ and peppermint+ herbal teas | alfalfa, roasted carob, marshmallow root, licorice root, roobios | hot, iced or sweet regular and decaf black tea, green tea and most herbal blends |
| Thyme | fresh, dried | | |
| Tofu | | fresh without preservatives or heavy spices | premade, preserved, flavored varieties |
| Tomatoes | | homegrown, yellow, low acid varieties | tomato sauce, paste, juice |
| Tortillas | corn, flour | | |
| Tums® | Tums® - Peppermint | Tums® - Tropical Fruit, Assorted Fruit flavors | Tums® - Sugar Free and citrus flavors |
| Turkey & Fowl | turkey, chicken, game hens | | heavily cured, preserved, smoked or spiced fowl products |
| Turmeric | | ground | |
| Turnips | fresh, organic | | |
| Vanilla | extract, bean pods | | |
| Veal | fresh or frozen | | heavily spiced, preserved or prepacked veal products |
| Vinegar | | | white, apple cider, red wine, |

| | Usually Bladder Friendly | Foods Worth Trying | Foods To Avoid |
|---|---|---|---|
| | | | balsamic, spirit |
| **Vitamins** | A, B1, B2, B12, D, E, K | low acid Ester C | Vitamin C & B6 |
| **Water** | tap or bottled, spring water | "essence" waters (i e MetroMint or Hint Waters) without sweeteners, colorings or artificial flavors | carbonated, "sparkling," vitamin, flavored and/or heavily filtered water |
| **Watercress** | | fresh | |
| **Watermelon** | | fresh | watermelon pickles |
| **Wheat Flour** | all purpose, bread, buckwheat, cake, pastry, semolina, whole-wheat | | |
| **Whipped Cream** | fresh whip cream, Cool Whip® | | |
| **White Wines** | none | Chardonnay, Pinot Grigio, Riesling, Sauvignon Blanc | Champagne, Sparkling Wines, Gewurztraminer, Muscat, Semillion |
| **Worcestershire Sauce** | | | worcestershire sauce - all brands |
| **Yogurt** | | plain, vanilla, blueberry, raspberry, peach or prune flavors | lemon, lime, orange, chocolate or mocha flavors, as well as yogurts that use aspartame or other artificial sugars |

# Appendix B

## What You Should Know About Food & Pesticides

*65% of produce samples tested positive for pesticides.*

Would you eat a piece of fruit if you knew that it contained pesticides? Would you give it to your child? A remarkable 65% of the thousands of produce samples analyzed by the US Department of Agriculture test positive for pesticide residues on the skin and in the flesh of the fruit. Pesticides persisted even after washing. For adults, pesticides have been linked to cancer and the development of endometriosis among other health effects. But for children, pesticides have been linked to decreased cognitive function, behav- ior problems and pediatric cancer. It's alarming.

Each year, the Environmental Working Group (EWG) conducts annual testing of produce and then releases the results in two important lists, the Dirty Dozen™ and the Clean Fifteen™. The newly released 2015 list offers good guidance and information that I believe is important to share. We must clean up our diets, not just from sugar but also harmful chemicals and pesticides, just as we must try to reduce chemical exposure in our homes.

### The Dirty Dozen™ 2015

Ninety nine percent of apple samples, 98% of peaches and 97% of nectarines tested positive for at least one pesticide residue. The average potato had more pesticides by weight than any other food. Amazingly, a single grape sample contained 15 pesticides. Single samples of cherry tomatoes, nectarines, peaches, imported snap peas and strawberries showed 13 different pesticides apiece.

- apples
- strawberries
- grapes
- celery
- peaches
- spinach
- sweet bell peppers
- nectarines
- cucumbers
- cherry tomatoes
- imported snap peas
- potatoes

Shocked? You should be. Can you imagine the pesticide load in the cheapest potatoes on the market today, the french fries found at most fast food outlets? They certainly aren't buying organic and, odds are, they are buying the cheapest potatoes that they can buy.

Are you a kale lover? You will be very disappointed to learn that kale, collard greens and hot peppers are on the Dirty Dozen PLUS™ list which highlights foods that contain trace levels of highly hazardous insecticides that are toxic to the human nervous system. They encourage customers who like these specific foods to only buy organic versions instead.

The Clean Fifteen™ highlights produce least likely to contain pesticide residue. Avocados, for example, were the cleanest with only one percent of avocado samples showing any detectable pesticides. Some 89 percent of pineapples, 82 percent of kiwi, 80 percent of papayas, 88 percent of mango and 61 percent of cantaloupe had no residues. Only 5.5% of the Clean Fifteen™ had two or more pesticides.

These safest foods included:
- avocados
- sweet corn
- pineapples ⌒
- cabbage
- frozen sweet peas
- onions ⌒
- asparagus
- mangoes ⌒
- papayas ⌒
- kiwi ⌒
- eggplant
- grapefruit ⌒
- cantaloupe
- cauliflower
- sweet potatoes

Now, of course, some of these aren't particularly bladder friendly. We certainly can not encourage the use of pineapples, grapefruit or Kiwi which can be quite irritating. But the others are worth trying.

As you browse your supermarket shelves, look at the labels closely. Yesterday, for example, I found a packet of veggie chips at my local Safeway store. I was shocked to see that it was produced in Vietnam. My preference is to support the American farming community who must follow FDA laws about pesticide use. I am also very cautious of foods produced in China where chemical and heavy metal contamination is rampant in both the rivers and soil. If you have no choice but to buy imported foods, hedge your bets by purchasing organic. Of course, the best fruit and veggies around are those produced in your own garden where you know how they have been treated and grown.

Learn more on the Environmental Working Group website: www.ewg.org.

# Appendix C

## "What if foods don't bother my bladder?"

If your bladder symptoms do not get worse after eating certain foods OR you do not struggle with pain BEFORE urination that suggests that your bladder wall is healthy. If, on the other hand, your pain is worse AFTER urination, your bladder symptoms may be originating in the pelvic floor muscles rather than the bladder wall. Ask your urologist or OB/GYN for a pelvic floor assessment to determine if you have pelvic floor dysfunction (aka tight muscles, trigger points, etc.) I think it would be wise to avoid some of the strong risk foods, particularly coffees, teas and sodas, until your diagnosis is clarified. Bladder wall irritation and pelvic floor tension often co-exist and patients may sometimes have bladder wall flares or pelvic floor flares. Your short and long-term goal is to protect the bladder wall.

## "Should I buy organic fruits and veggies?"

When it's possible and affordable, we encourage you to buy organic. Why? Research has proven that pesticides linger not only on the skin but in the meat of various fruits and vegetables. Each year, the Environmental Working Group releases a list of Dirty Dozen™ and Clean Fifteen™ foods that are worth reviewing. Pound for pound, for example, potatoes contain the highest amounts of pesticides and, at this point, it's best to buy organic. On the other hand, avocados tested the cleanest of all the foods tested. You can learn more about this in Appendix B.

## "How much water should I drink?"

Until the bladder wall heals, patients must remember that their bladder is injured and more vulnerable. Unfortunately some patients cut back on their water intake, allowing their urine to become more concentrated and irritating. Urine should be a pale, clear yellow. If urine is dark yellow or cloudy, that suggests that the patient is dehydrated and they should drink more water. If urine is clear, then the patient has gone too far and could be compromising their electrolyte levels. Just drink a normal 6 to 8 glasses of water a day. IC patients generally prefer to sip a glass of water over time rather chugging a large glass of water.

## "I'm afraid to eat anything. What should I do?"

There's no reason to fear food. Rather, fear the food manufacturers who process foods so aggressively that they rarely resemble the real thing and are far more likely to irritate the bladder. Go back to the basics: simple, fresh healthy foods. Try the least bothersome foods from the LIU food list or the foods listed in the Bladder Friendly category of the ICN Food List. An ideal breakfast, for example, would be scrambled eggs and hash browns. Homemade pancakes or waffles could work, ideally served with butter and some bladder friendly jam or real, homemade syrup rather than the preservative filled commercial brands. Looking for an easy lunch? How about a sandwich made with nitrate free turkey or chicken. The Boar's Head brand is a great choice. You'll find many dinner and dessert ideas in this cookbook as well!

## "I react to some foods on the Bladder Friendly/Safe list. Why?"

The IC diet is very individual depending on the degree of inflammation/injury of the bladder wall. Patients with more mild IC can tolerate more foods while patients with more severe irritation and/or

Hunner's lesions may have a more reactive bladder. Some patients may also have pre-existing allergies and/or food sensitivities that they must respect and avoid. As the bladder receives treatment and begins to improve, foods should be better tolerated. If you have struggled with food sensitivities, you might want to consider having food sensitivity testing (i.e. ALCAT) to help isolate those foods which are irritating your body.

### "Why can I eat a food one day and, a few days later, flare from it?"

This is common and related to the level of irritation and inflammation of your bladder wall which, unfortunately, can change on a daily basis. If you've been following the IC diet and your bladder is calming down, it's normal to start trying some of the riskier foods. On the first day, that soda didn't cause a noticeable reaction though, at the cellular level. it may have triggered some new inflammation. The second day, you enjoy another one and it still seems okay but you've triggered another round of inflammation. After you drink your third soda, your bladder starts screaming. That's due to the cumulative toll of irritation and inflammation of all of the foods you've eaten in that specific period of time.

### "Why does my food tolerance vary with my menstrual cycle?"

The bladder wall and urethra is extremely responsive to hormone swings thus women frequently struggle with flares the day that they ovulate or a few days before their period. Because the tissues are just more sensitive at those times, you will probably eat more bladder safe foods.

### "I feel like I react to every food. What should I do?"

Patients who struggle with severe bladder wall inflammation and/or Hunner's lesions may feel like every food bothers them. It doesn't mean that the food is causing their IC. It means that their bladder wall is profoundly irritated and inflamed. Hunner's lesions, for example, require very specific treatment (fulguration, laser therapy or injection of triamcinolone) that can dramatically reduce pain and discomfort. You may need to do more IC treatments to help calm down the inflammation so that you can start eating more food comfortably. Please refer to the treatment section of the IC Network website for additional information on the AUA's six step IC treatment protocol.

### "I can't live without my soda. What should I do?"

Make no mistake. Your addiction to soda is not your fault. Those companies deliberately use high amounts of sugar and high fructose corn syrup to make you addicted so that you will be a return customer. Some compare the addictive power of sugar to that of cocaine. The soda industry doesn't care that their products come with a physical price, drives obesity and is a leading cause of diabetes. In their minds, profit is more important than your health. If that doesn't infuriate you then consider what the high levels of acid found in soda will do to a wound in your bladder. It will make the irritation and inflammation far worse and, if used repeatedly, could make wounds bigger. Try a sparkling water with a little bit of soda flavoring instead. That's much more bladder friendly and will give you that sensation of soda without the acid. Rather than being a pawn to the soda industry who could care less about our family and our health, I think we need to fight back and not buy their products anymore. Most of all, we should never introduce soda to young children.

### "Coffee in the morning helps me have a bowel movement. What should I do?"

It's true. Coffee helps millions of people have a comfortable bowel movement in the morning but so can a good breakfast. The bowel works via a "food in, poop out" process, also known as peristalsis. When you eat, gentle muscle contractions progress through the bowel to move food along and eventually out. In fact, it's actually pretty difficult to have a bowel movement before you eat or drink in the morning. Eating and drinking triggers peristalsis. Thus, it's better to have a good breakfast followed with a mug of something hot to get that started. I usually drink a roasted roobios herbal tea with great success yet without the bladder irritation from the coffee!

## "I've lived on junk food. It's what I've always eaten but now it hurts. What can I do?"

For some patients, a diagnosis of IC is a wake up call. Your body is saying that it's been hurt and needs your attention. Junk food is just that, junk. It has little nutritional value and will not give your body the essential nutrients it needs to heal and function normally. The pain of IC can be a powerful source of motivation to eat better. Don't waste years like IC patient Judy who I mentioned in our introduction. She suffered needlessly because of her addiction to coffee and soda. Instead ask yourself "How can I help a wound in my bladder heal?" Then focus on those foods that aren't irritating.

## "I'm not a cook. I don't really know how to cook, what should I do?"

You're missing out on a wonderful hobbie. The good news is that cookbooks like this will give you lots of fun recipes to play with. Just experiment and look for flavors that you enjoy. It takes trial and error but you can do it. You'll also find some fabulous recipes in the IC Cookbooks and cruising Pinterest where you can see great pictures of what it will look like. Also, look for classes at local kitchen stores (i.e. Sur La Table) or community colleges. We all have to start somewhere and classes are a great way to meet other people!

## "Some acidic foods, like lemon, become alkaline in the body. Shouldn't I eat these?"

No, you shouldn't. Yes, we say avoid acidic foods because these are easy for patients to identify. But some of the strong acid foods do become strongly alkaline during the digestive process. But, as I often say, bleach is just as damaging as sulfuric acid. Our goal here is to avoid pH extremes, whether they be acidic or alkaline. Rather we want to try to eat more pH neutral foods.

## "Should I drink alkaline water?"

Some patients make the mistake of only drinking alkaline water which, as I say in the previous question, can be damaging as alkalinity levels rise. So, no, I do not believe that alkaline water should be drunk in any large quantity. If you've eaten something acidic and want to neutralize it, you can use the OTC supplement Prelief, some TUMS or, perhaps, a small glass of alkaline water. But, drinking it every day is excessive and expensive. The best water to drink is simple Spring Water or tap water if its' not heavily treated. Some patients also prefer Fiji or Evian Water.

## "Is juicing safe for IC?"

Juicing needs to be approached with caution because it forces you to eat a much higher quantity of certain fruits and vegetables than you normally would if you were eating whole fruit. Obviously, you can't use any of the citrus fruits, nor should you be using the tart or bitter apples fruits. On the other hand, you may enjoy using the lower acid fruits. I often enjoy banana, mango, peach or blueberry smoothies made with apple juice and a lot of ice.

# Appendix D

## More Books on the IC Diet

### A Taste of the Good Life: A Cookbook for an IC Diet

The first diet book created for patients struggling with IC, it is still one of our most popular & practical books! Author Bev Laumann provides an extensive, thoroughly researched resource for patients seeking information on diet and nutrition. Half educational book and half fabulous bladder recipes, you'll find lots of tips and suggestions on how to make low acid coffees, find low acid wines, the vulvodynia oxalate diet and more! Even the appendices are chock full of useful information, particularly the one that discusses vitamins and lists all the foods that you can eat to increase your vitamin intake. This book is perfect for foodies and patients who love to cook!

### Confident Choices®: Customizing the IC Diet

Witten by Julie Beyer, RD, Confident Choices®: Customizing the IC diet offers fifteen comprehensive chapters covering a variety of topics including flare foods, discovering your trigger foods, planning meals, ideas for breakfast, lunch and dinner, some IC friendly recipes, dietary supplements, exercise & fitness and IC diet success stories. If you're stumped about what to eat or why you should avoid it, this book will answer the great majority of your questions.

### Confident Choices®: A Cookbook for IC & OAB

Confident Choices®: A Cookbook for IC and Overactive Bladder is ideal for patients who want the information short and sweet. Author Julie Beyer RD walks the novice patient through essential IC diet basics in a style that is simple, easy to understand and inherently practical. It is a perfect resource for patients who are afraid to eat for fear of causing an IC flare. The section on rescue menus alone will be greatly appreciated by patients currently struggling with a sensitive bladder. With a positive and encouraging tone and style, Julie reminds her readers about key nutrition basics and offers short, concise discussions. She offers an excellent list of IC friendly food substitutions. For example, pear or blueberry juice can be used in place of lemon juice or vinegar in many recipes. She includes a step by step guide on how to do an elimination diet to determine which, if any, foods you are sensitive to. She offers a wide variety of recipes for breakfast, snacks and appetizers, soups, salads, breads, main dishes, vegetables, pasta, desserts, candies and beverages. One new and great idea she includes is a printable shopping list of IC friendly foods that patients can take to the grocery store to make good, informed decisions about their diet.

### Interstitial Cystitis: A Guide For Nutrition Educators

The first book written for dietitians and other nutrition educators, this book the latest rescarch, a modified elimination diet technique plus helpful resources specifically written for nutrition professionals. Written by Julie Beyer, RD.

### The Happy Bladder Cookbook

Written in 2010 by IC patient Mia Eliot, the Happy Bladder Cookbook offers 75+ flavorful and creative recipes that are compliant with the 2009 IC/PBS Diet Food List. If you're looking new fresh flavors, tastes and ideas to liven up your diet, this is a lovely addition to your IC cookbooks. At 24 years of age,

Mia has had her share of health challenges, including a diagnosis of IC in 2008. While she was struggling with her new diagnosis and losing her job, Mia went back to her old passion: cooking. This cookbook shares some of her favorite recipes adapted to the IC friendly diet and represents her desire to turn lemons into lemonade. Well not actually lemonade since it's very irritating. The fact is that she is extremely positive and encouraging. The book is available via pdf or in print.

## The Happy Bladder Christmas Cookbook

Mia Eliot's holiday cookbook offers 75+ flavorful and creative bladder friendly recipes for pastries, candies, cookies, cakes, pies and much more!  If you love breakfast, you'll be inspired by the 14 new recipes she offers, including frittata's, cinnamon rolls, cinnamon streusel muffins, gingerbread French toast and pumpkin gingersnap waffles. The cookies will make for a lovely afternoon baking with children and/or for your family. Try the sweet and salty caramel nut pretzel bars! Looking for a special cake to bring to your family celebrations? She offers recipes for cheesecakes, layer cakes and traditional holiday favorites like gingerbread and poppy seed. And, for those days when you need a little comfort, you can't go wrong with creme brulee, almond peer crisp and floating islands! This book is only available via pdf file (electronic format).

## IC Friendly Fit & Fresh

In her third cookbook, IC patient Mia Elliot shares 75 new tasty, flavorful IC friendly recipes that are also kind to our waistline. Each are under 500 calories!  Her breakfast selections include oatmeals, waffles, smoothies, has and a frittata. If you love soup, salad and sandwiches you'll love her new offerings!  Missing Pizza? You can enjoy it following her creative recipes. Also includes a variety of main dishes, side dishes and, of course, desserts.  Available in print and as a pdf file.  Kindle version is available through Amazon.

## All of these books are available through the ICN Shop at: http://www.icnsales.com/diet-nutrition/

# Appendix E

## Fighting Constipation With Fiber

Because interstitial cystitis patients often struggle with irritable bowel syndrome and constipation, maintaining a diet high in fiber is important. My IBS specialist recommended eating 20 to 24 grams of fiber per day to have normal, comfortable bowel movements. I was shocked to discover that I was only eating 8 grams of fiber a day. No wonder I was struggling.

Another challenge lay in the type of fiber consumed. Insoluble fibers, such as fibers found in most bran cereals and leafy greens, can be heavy, rough in texture and be more irritating our tender GI tract. Twenty grams of this type of fiber can leave the patient more bloated, irritated and crampy. In contrast, soluble fibers that dissolve more easily in water are gentler on the gut. So, if you're looking to load fiber by using heavy cereals, you might find yourself more uncomfortable. Try, instead, more naturally derived fibers from the following list of foods.

If you're using a fiber supplement, look for soluble fibers that dissolve in water, such as Heather's Tummy Acacia Fiber. Though popular, psyllium husk products contain some insoluble fiber which can irritate.

### Peas

> ½ cup peas – 9.1 grams
> 1 cup cooked peas – 13.4 grams

### Apples (please use lower acid Gala or Fuji )

> Medium size raw  - 4.0 grams of fiber
> Baked apple – 5.0 grams of fiber

### Artichoke

> 1 large cooked – 4.5 grams of fiber

### Banana

> 1 medium – 3 grams of fiber

### Beans

> 1 cup northern beans – 16 grams of fiber
> 1 cup cooked kidney beans – 19.4 grams (can be gassy)
> ½ cup Lima Beans – 5.8 grams
> 1 cup cooked pinto beans – 18.8 grams
> ½ cup white beans – 8.0 grams
> 1 cup cooked garbanzo beans – 12 grams
> 1 8 oz. can of baked beans – 16 grams

## Breads

2 slices Ezekiel (by Food For Life) bread – 6 grams of fiber

2 slices 7 grain bread – 6.5 grams of fiber

## Broccoli

¾ cup cooked broccoli – 7 grams of fiber

½ cup raw broccoli – 4 grams

## Carrots

½ cup cooked carrots – 3.4 grams of fiber

## Corn

1 medium ear of corn on the cob – 5 grams of fiber

½ cup cooked kernels or cream style – 5 grams

## Pear

1 medium pear – 4 grams of fiber

## Potatoes

1 medium Idaho baked potato – 5 grams of fiber

1 medium boiled potato – 3.5 grams of fiber

½ cup of mashed potato – 3.0 grams

1 small sweet potato – 4 grams of fiber

## Rice

½ cup white rice – 2.0 grams

½ cup brown rice – 5.5 grams

## Spinach

½ cup cooked spinach – 7 grams of fiber

1 cup raw spinach – 3.5 grams of fiber

(*high in oxalates)

## Squash

½ cup summer squash – 2.0 grams

½ cup winter squash (baked or mashed) – 3.5 grams

## Turnips

½ cup white turnip cooked – 2 grams of fiber

½ cup yellow turnip cooked – 3.2 grams of fiber

Adapted From The Mount Sinai Bowel Function & Dietary Fiber Chart
https://www.wehealny.org/healthinfo/dietaryfiber/fibercontentchart.html

# Appendix F

## Fatigue Fighting Foods

Are you struggling with fatigue?? If you're like many, you may have relied caffeine and fast carbs for a quick energy boost. The problem? They'll give you a quick burst of energy but two hours later leave you feeling tired, brain fogged and craving yet more carbs.

Maintaining steady and consistent energy levels require eating less rapidly digested carbs (sugars, breads, pastas) and more proteins and healthy fats. The goal is to avoid the rapid blood sugar fluctuations that steal your energy. But here's another tidbit you might not know. Chronic fatigue has been linked to high levels of inflammation in the body, thus eating foods which fight inflammation (i.e. antioxidants, omega-3 fatty acids) can also help! Here are foods that can have you running on cruise control all day long!

## Water

Get into the habit of drinking 6 to 8 glasses of water a day. Mild dehydration has been linked to a reduction in mood, energy levels and mental functioning! When you start craving sugar, drink a glass of water first!

## Eggs

Start your day with eggs! This high protein food provides essential B vitamins and choline, a substance critical in reducing inflammation throughout the body. Choline helps boost brain health and functioning. It is also used to make acetylcholine, an essential neurotransmitter in our nervous system. Anything that improves both brain and nerve function can help us be more alert.

## Whole Grains

Unlike white bread, whole grains contain complex carbohydrates that release energy throughout the day! If you struggle with gluten sensitivity, look for the many, new gluten free breads on the market today!

## Blueberries

Loaded with antioxidants, blueberries are a staple in most IC patients diets. A study published in the Annals of Neurology suggests that antioxidant-rich blueberries can reduce cognitive decline in older adults by up to 2.5 years. Antioxidants help with cognitive function and mental agility! The great news is that they are low in sugar, making them an excellent snack for diabetics as well.

## Almonds

Bladder and stomach friendly, almonds are high in protein, fiber, healthy monounsaturated fats, magnesium, vitamin E and calcium. Eating almonds can help fight inflammation, lower LDL cholesterol, lower blood pressure and sustain energy throughout the day.

## Popcorn

High in fiber, low in calories, homemade popcorn is a healthier snack and a great source of energy! Avoid the prepackaged, sweet or flavored popcorns that contain high amounts of sugar and, worse, artificial colorings and flavorings!

## Broccoli & Spinach

High in vitamin C, lutein, beta carotene and fiber, broccoli contains potent anti-inflammatory and antioxidants. Spinach is an excellent source of vitamin A, iron, folate, vitamin C, magnesium, selenium, zinc, niacin and riboflavin.

## Sweet Potatoes

Sweet potatoes contain mostly complex carbohydrates that don't cause sudden spikes in blood sugar. High in fiber, B6, C, E, folate and potassium, sweet potatoes make an excellent snack, such as Danielle's organic sweet potato chips!

## Salmon

Salmon contains high levels of omega 3 fatty acids that have a potent anti-inflammatory effect. Eating salmon and other Omega-3 foods ell known to elevate your mood and fight depression.

## Grass Fed Beef

Unlike beef fed on grains, grass-fed beef is leaner, richer in protein, vitamins, minerals and omega-3 fats. Beef is also the best form of iron in our diet.

## Low Acid Coffee

Coffee is popular for a reason, it can help increase energy and alertness when used in SMALL quantities and without the sugar or milk based flavorings. The challenge is that it's relying on chemistry rather than good nutrition to maintain your health. If you have to use it, use a very small mount, preferably a LOW ACID coffee with Prelief instead!

# Appendix G

## Five-Step Coffee Challenge

Not sure if you're ready to drink coffee again? Here's our five-step hot drink challenge that we suggest to every patient considering drinking coffee again. Start at Step One and slowly work your way down. If any of these trigger your symptoms, then stop and go back up a step. If your bladder tolerates one well, then proceed to the next step and give it a try. Please note, however, that whenever you're struggling with active symptoms, it's best to keep your hot drinks mild and simple! (i.e. one through three)

**Step One: Hot water or milk!** *(Mild flavorings optional: vanilla, caramel, etc.)*

**Step Two: Chamomile & Peppermint Herbal Teas**

**Step Three: Rooibos Herbal Teas**

**Step Four: Herbal Coffee (<u>Pero</u>, <u>Kaffree Roma</u> or <u>Cafix</u>)**

**Step Five: Low Acid Coffee**
If you've passed all of the previous steps and your bladder tolerates them well, then it's time to try the real thing but there's a catch! You need to try LOW ACID coffee. These are grown at lower altitudes, tend to be darker roasts and, ideally, should be brewed using a cold brew process (i.e. <u>The Toddy Coffee Maker</u>) to make a genuine low acid coffee!

We love <u>Simpatico Low Acid Coffee</u> for its flavor and acidity level! This small company based in Holland MI has made the crafting of low acid coffee an art form,.with great flavors, mouth feel and satisfaction. Buy now them in the ICN Shop – www.icnsales.com

## About Interstitial Cystitis

Interstitial cystitis (IC), also known as painful bladder syndrome, bladder pain syndrome, hypersensitive bladder syndrome or chronic pelvic pain syndrome, is a condition that results in recurring discomfort or pain in the bladder and the surrounding pelvic region. The symptoms can vary greatly between individuals and even for the same person throughout the month, including an urgent need to urinate (urgency), a frequent need to urinate (frequency) and, for some, pressure and/or pelvic pain. People with severe cases of IC/BPS may urinate as many as 60 times a day, including frequent nighttime urination (nocturia).

Pain levels can range from mild tenderness to intense, agonizing pain. Pain typically worsens as the bladder fills and is then relieved after urination. Pain may also radiate to the lower back, upper legs, vulva and penis. Women's symptoms may fluctuate with their menstrual cycle, often flaring during ovulation and/or just before their periods. Men and women may experience discomfort during or after sexual relations.

IC affects patients of all ages, races and cultures. It is found on every continent in the world. Though it was previously thought to be a disease affecting mostly women, new studies suggest that men suffering from chronic non-bacterial prostatitis may also have IC, thus dramatically expanding the population data. It is not unusual for IC to run in families nor for patients to struggle with a syndrome of related conditions including: IBS, anxiety disorder, vulvodynia, pelvic floor dysfunction, allergies, migraines and fibromyalgia. There are many treatments and self-help strategies now available that can help improve bladder symptoms dramatically. One excellent place to gather information is on the IC Network website (http://www.ic-network.com), where you can read extensive articles on IC as well as participate in our support forum and chats.

## About the IC Network

Founded in 1994, the Interstitial Cystitis Network is a health education and social advocacy company dedicated to interstitial cystitis and other pelvic pain disorders. Our mission is to present the best research, information, and support directly into the homes and offices of our users (patients, providers & IC researchers).

In addition to our magazine, the **IC Optimist**, and our free e-newsletters, the ICN offers comprehensive support services for patients throughout the world, including the ICN support forum (www.ic-network.com/forum/), our patient assistance phone line and the **"Living with IC"** educational video series currently available on YouTube (www.youtube.com/icnjill/).

Led by IC patient and activist Jill Heidi Osborne, the ICN received the highest score and recommendation from researchers at the University of London (2013) who conducted a review of the accuracy, credibility, readability of IC/BPS websites, outpacing all other non-profit and government websites. In 2011, a similar study conducted by Harvard Medical School rated **Medscape** and the **IC Network** the two highest quality websites dedicated to IC. We've received the **Wellsphere Health Award**, the **Netwellness Consumer Health Information Award**, a coveted five star review from **ObGyn.Net**, a four star review from **Mentalhealth.net** and others. We prove, on a daily basis, that disabled patients have much to give the IC community and the world at large.

Visit us today at:
www.ic-network.com
www.icawareness.org
www.ketaminecystitis.org
www.icdietproject.com
www.painfulbladder.com

<u>Notes</u>